Authors in Their Age

The Age of
KEATS and SHELLEY

Authors in Their Age

The Age of
KEATS and SHELLEY

Heather Coombs

BLACKIE

BLACKIE & SON LTD
Bishopbriggs Glasgow G64 2NZ
450 Edgware Road London W2 1EG

Printed in Great Britain by Thomson Litho Ltd, East Kilbride, Scotland

Authors in Their Age

Authors in Their Age is a series of introductions to the work of major authors in English literature. Each book provides the background information that can help a reader see such an author in context, involved in and reacting to the society of which he was a part.

Some volumes are devoted to individual authors such as Chaucer and Wordsworth. Others look at a particular period in our literary history in which an author can be seen as representative of his time— for example, *The Age of Keats and Shelley* and *The Age of Lawrence*.

There is no attempt to impose a standard format on each of the books. However, all the books provide biographical material and deal with the important political, social and cultural movements of the time. Each book considers the author's readership, the problems of editing his or her work and the major influences on his or her writing. All are well illustrated with drawings, documents or photographs of the time.

There is also a guide to further reading and other source material which will enable the student to progress to a more detailed study of the writer's work and its treatment by literary critics.

Anthony Adams
Esmor Jones
General Editors

Contents

I

Towards a Biography of Keats

John Keats was born on 31 October, 1795, the eldest of four children. His father, Thomas, who was in charge of livery stables attached to an inn, died in a riding accident in April, 1804, at the age of thirty, leaving his widow with four small children—John, George, born in 1797, Tom, born in 1799, and a baby girl of ten months, Frances.

The widow was far from inconsolable. Less than three months later she remarried, and the following summer the Keats children went to live with their grandmother in Edmonton.

All three boys attended Clarke's School in Enfield, and John became friendly with Charles Cowden Clarke, son of the headmaster. This school at least provided some sort of secure background, for family life was somewhat irregular; Keats' mother, now Mrs Rawlings, had abandoned her husband in 1806 and eventually returned to live with her children. But in March, 1810, Keats was told at school that his mother had died of tuberculosis.

Keats had until then been making very promising progress at the school. He had been reading widely, including such liberal papers as *The Examiner*, encouraged by Charles Cowden Clarke, and this friendship continued after Keats left the school in summer, 1810. In that year Keats' grandmother put her money in trust for the Keats children, and one of the trustees, Mr Abbey, a warehouseman, was made their guardian. George Keats was removed from the school to be a clerk in Abbey's business, and John was bound apprentice for five years to a surgeon in Edmonton named Hammond.

Sometime in 1813–14, John Keats quarrelled with Mr Hammond, and ceased to lodge in his house, as had been the previous arrangement. Tom Keats and John moved into lodgings together.

At this time, John was first introduced to the glories of the poet, Spenser. He read avidly 'Epithalamium' and *The Faerie Queene* and produced his first attempt at poetry—'Imitation of Spenser'.

Although poetry was occupying his mind more and more, Keats had by no means yet decided on a full-time career as a poet. Although he had broken with Hammond, medicine was still to be his vocation, and in 1815 he registered for surgical training at Guy's Hospital. However, he was simultaneously broadening his interest in the arts, and at this time became friendly with the poet, George Felton Mathew, and the artist, Joseph Severn.

In spite of the legend that Keats was never keen on his medical studies, in July, 1816, he passed the difficult examinations to receive the licence of the Society of Apothecaries; he seemed to have a promising career ahead of him, for he had been appointed dresser to a surgeon at Guy's. But in the autumn of 1816 he informed Abbey—no longer his guardian after 31 October, 1816, for Keats was then twenty-one—that he was giving up medicine for poetry.

At this time Keats met the poet, John Hamilton Reynolds, to whom he later wrote some of his finest letters; he was also introduced by Cowden Clarke to Leigh Hunt, editor of the radical paper, *The Examiner*, at whose house he was to meet Shelley.

Keats now began to devote himself earnestly to poetry. In the winter of 1816 he wrote his first composition of any length, 'Sleep and Poetry', in which he dedicates himself to the pursuit of poetry and asks for:

> *ten years, that I may overwhelm*
> *Myself in poesy; so I may do the deed*
> *That my own soul has to itself decreed.*[1]

It was a request that was not to be granted.

A determination to write a longer work led him in April, 1817, to travel to the Isle of Wight to work in quiet surroundings, for he had been sharing lodgings with George and Tom for some months. At first he was all enthusiasm, writing to Reynolds, *'I find I cannot exist without poetry—without eternal poetry'*, and adding, *'I shall forthwith begin my Endymion'*.[2] But within a month he had moved to Margate, where he shared lodgings with Tom, and was writing to Leigh Hunt:

> *I went to the Isle of Wight—thought so much about Poetry so long together that I could not get to sleep at night.*[3]

By October, with the end of 'Endymion' in sight, Keats regarded it merely as *'a test, a trial of my Powers of Imagination'*, adding somewhat tartly, *'I must make 4000 lines of one bare circumstance and fill them with Poetry'*. Even so, he still regarded this as *'a great task'* and felt that:

> *a long Poem is a test of invention. . . . Did our great Poets ever write short Pieces?*[4]

1. *John Keats* by B. R. Haydon, 1816. John Keats was sketched by the artist, Benjamin Robert Haydon, in 1816, at the start of his poetic career. Haydon's perpetual money worries eventually became a problem to Keats. (National Portrait Gallery, London)

During the summer of 1817 Keats had met three people who were to remain close friends with him. They were Mr and Mrs Charles Dilke, and their neighbour, Charles Brown, who lived in the two halves of Wentworth Place, a house in Hampstead. Also at this time he became acquainted with Benjamin Bailey, a young man who was at Oxford University studying to take holy orders. Bailey suggested that Keats should spend September with him at Magdalen Hall. Here Keats found a delightful atmosphere of study—indeed, he teased Bailey about his voracious appetite for reading:

> *I should not like to be Pages in your way when in a tolerable hungry mood you have no Mercy.*[5]

However, 'Endymion' was still not finished, and once again, Keats sought seclusion to try to complete it. Staying at an inn near Box Hill, he managed to finish the poem in November, 1817.

Keats returned to London, and found that one of his heroes was there—the poet Wordsworth. Keats' attitude to Wordsworth vacillated later, and his early *'Reverence'* turned to dislike for poetry *'that has a palpable design upon us'*.[6] But, in 1817, Keats was delighted when his friend the painter Robert Haydon arranged a meeting with the great man. Keats now seemed to be fulfilling his desire of living for poetry, moving in circles where he met writers and poets such as Wordsworth, Shelley, Hunt and Lamb.

But in January, 1818, Tom started coughing up blood, and it became obvious that he had tuberculosis. The disease was then thought to be hereditary, and the sonnet Keats wrote in this month, 'When I have fears that I may cease to be', sums up his only too well-founded fears of early death *'Before my pen has glean'd my teeming brain'*.

Also in January, 1818, however, Keats found time to attend a series of lectures by the writer and critic Hazlitt, called *On the English Poets*. Like Hazlitt, Keats was a fervent admirer of Shakespeare, and, on 23 January, in a letter to his brother at Teignmouth, in Devon, where Tom had gone for the sake of his health, Keats wrote the sonnet 'On Sitting Down to Read King Lear Once Again'. Both in the situation of Lear himself and in the lines referring to the *'old oak forest'* and the *'barren dream'*, there is a foretaste of the great work of the following year, 'Hyperion'.

However, practical concerns continued to obtrude themselves into Keats' life, and now, as so often, they were the concerns of his brothers. Tom could not be left alone at Teignmouth, and it would not be wise for him to return. But George wanted to go to London to make arrangements about his inheritance, for he was twenty-one at the end of February, 1818. Keats duly travelled down to Teignmouth to nurse his ailing brother. He found Tom *'low-spirited'*,[7] and the weather depressing, with continual rain, but still managed to feel altruistic enough to write to his publisher, Taylor:

> *I find that I can have no enjoyment in the World but continual drinking of knowledge—I find there is no worthy pursuit but the idea of doing some good for the world . . . there is but one way for me—the road lies through application study and thought.*[8]

2. *Lorenzo and Isabella* by Sir J. E. Millais, P.R.A. This illustration to Keats' poem, 'Isabella', is by one of a group of Victorian artists called 'The Pre-Raphaelites', who much admired his use of colour and interest in medievalism. (Walker Art Gallery, Liverpool)

One of the books he had been thinking about was Boccaccio's *Decameron*. This is a collection of stories actually written in the mid-fourteenth century by the Italian, Giovanni Boccaccio, but supposedly told to each other by a group of young men and women fleeing from the plague in Florence. The book had a great influence on English writers, especially Chaucer. Keats was interested in things medieval, as we shall see in Chapter 7, and before going to Devon he had started a poem—'Isabella, or the Pot of Basil'—based on a story from the Decameron. He followed Boccaccio's version fairly closely, but his avowed interest in *'doing some good for the world'* can be seen in the stanzas where he refers to Isabella's brothers. In the original story, we merely learn that they had become wealthy on the death of their father, but Keats uses the occasion to attack exploitation of workers:

> *And for them many a weary hand did swelt*
> *In torched mines and noisy factories,*
> *... for them alone did seethe*
> *A thousand men in troubles wide and dark:*
> *Half-ignorant, they turn'd an easy wheel,*
> *That set sharp racks at work, to pinch and peel.*[9]

During the spring of 1818, Keats was undecided over a plan he had made to tour the Lake District and Scotland. In April, he wrote to Haydon:

> *I purpose within a month to put my knapsack at my back and make a pedestrian tour through the north of England, and part of Scotland ...*[10]

But in his letter to Taylor at the end of the month, he indicated that he might not go, as he had not spent enough time studying. Three days later he told Reynolds, *'I shall perhaps remain here* [Teignmouth] *for some Months'*.[11]

In the following month, however, he definitely decided to go on the walking tour, with Charles Brown, the friend from Hampstead. Brown had decided that, while he was away touring the north, he would let his half of Wentworth Place, and the tenants were to be Mrs Brawne, a widow, and her three children, Fanny, Samuel and Margaret. Brown could have had little idea, when he made the plan, what exquisite pain and delight this arrangement was to bring to his friend Keats later that year.

Meanwhile, however, before setting out on the walking tour, Keats was involved in a very important family occasion. His brother George had decided:

> *to emigrate to the back settlements of America, become farmer and work with his own hands after purchasing 1400 hundred Acres of the American Government.*[12]

Keats would not have been happy at the idea of George going alone, but wrote:

> *he will marry before he sets sail a young lady he has known some years—of a nature liberal and highspirited enough to follow him to the Banks of the Mississippi.*[13]

The young lady was called Georgiana Augusta Wylie, and she met with Keats' entire approval; he later wrote to her:

> *I have a tenderness for you; and an admiration which I feel to be as great and more chaste than I can have for any woman in the world.*[14]

George and Georgiana were married in May, 1818. In June, they travelled with Keats and Brown to Liverpool, and from there they sailed to America. Keats and Brown travelled on, further north, to begin their walking tour. They arrived at Windermere on 26 June, 1818, and Keats announced, on seeing the Lakes, *'they surpass my expectations'.*[15] He was, however, rather disillusioned by Wordsworth, who:

> *instead of being in retirement has himself and his house full in the thick of fashionable visitors quite convenient to be pointed at all summer long.*[16]

Keats and Brown moved on from Ambleside, at the northern end of Windermere, to Rydal, and hence further north to Keswick. They walked strenuously, covering a great deal of ground. On 29 June, Keats wrote to Tom:

> *So we have walked ten miles before Breakfast today. We . . . felt, on arising into the cold air, that same elevation which a cold bath gives one. I felt as if I were going to a Tournament.*[17]

By 1 July, they were at Carlisle, and travelled from there to Dumfries and on into Kirkcudbrightshire. They suddenly decided that it would not take long to visit the Giant's Causeway, and so set sail for Ireland from Portpatrick, on the west coast of Scotland. They did not see the Giant's Causeway, but they did encounter grinding poverty, which left an ineradicable impression on Keats, who described:

> *the worse than nakedness, the rags, the dirt and misery of the poor common Irish.*

He added miserably:

> *What a tremendous difficulty is the improvement of the condition of such people . . . with me it is absolute despair.*[18]

Returning to Scotland after their short excursion to Ireland, Keats and Brown travelled further north to visit the cottage of the poet Burns at Alloway, near Ayr. They were still travelling considerable distances by coach and on foot—'*20 miles a day in general*'.[19] In mid-July, they reached Loch Lomond, went north and west to Inveraray, and then on to Loch Craignish. By the end of July, they were conscious of extreme discomfort, finding only wretched accommodation with coarse food. '*Poor Brown*' had blistered feet, and the weather was miserable. Even so, they pushed on, and Keats wrote of walking '*15 miles in a soaking rain*'.[20] In spite of his small stature—he described himself as '*Mister John Keats five feet high*'[21] —he seemed to be coping admirably with the strain of '*four months tramping in the highlands*'.[22]

By the end of July they were at Oban, visited Mull and saw Fingal's Cave and Iona, but now, for the first time, there was a hint that all might not be well. In a letter to Tom, Keats indicates that he has a slight sore throat, but within three days, he says it is '*getting quite well*'[23]—well enough to go up Ben Nevis. By 6 August, when he wrote to George's mother-in-law, Mrs Wylie, they were in Inverness. But then the throat became worse, and Keats was forced to alter his plans; he felt ill enough to abandon the tour, take ship for Cromarty, and head for home. He arrived in London on 17 August, and there bad news awaited him; he was not the only invalid. Tom had been ill during Keats' absence, '*and for the last fortnight*', Keats wrote to their sister Fanny, '*has been worse than ever.*'[24]

For the next three-and-a-half months, Keats was constantly nursing Tom. Yet, amazingly, this was a time of great creative power for him. In September, 1818, he began what must surely count as his first great work, 'Hyperion'. This vision of the overthrow of the old order of gods, the Titans, by the new generation, including the new poet-god, Apollo, is an expression of Keats' own endeavour to fulfil his '*powers of poetry*' and to be among the '*English Poets*'.[25] It was a theme which he was to rework in a far more personal manner the following year, in 'The Fall of Hyperion'.

Tom's early death, at the age of nineteen, on 1 December, 1818, was to have a profound effect upon Keats. The idea of death wasting away the young and the beautiful occurs frequently in Keats' poetry hereafter—in 'La Belle Dame sans Merci', for example, where the knight-at-arms has a pale brow '*with anguish moist and fever dew*'; or in 'Ode on Melancholy', where Melancholy dwells with '*Beauty that must die*'; or in 'Ode to a Nightingale', where Keats describes this world '*Where youth grows pale and spectre-thin and dies*'.

After Tom's death, Keats went to live with Brown in Wentworth Place. Sometime before this, however, Keats had become acquainted

with Fanny Brawne, daughter of the widow who had rented Brown's house for the summer. The Brawnes had moved from Wentworth Place when Brown returned, but were still living in the neighbourhood. By 4 January, 1819, when writing to George and Georgiana, Keats describes Fanny as:

> *beautiful and elegant, graceful, silly, fashionable and strange we have a little tiff now and then.*[26]

He goes on to paint her in more detail, adding that her behaviour is *'monstrous . . . flying out in all directions'*. He feels this is not from:

> *any innate vice but from a penchant she has for acting stylishly. I am however tired of such style and shall decline any more of it.*[27]

But he did not keep this resolution.

Meanwhile, Keats was concerned with money worries, which were to plague him continually from this time. Haydon was pressing for money, and Keats, while promising to *'sacrifice everything I have to your service'*, begged him *'let me be the last stay—ask the rich lovers of art first.'*[28]

However, his problems did not keep him from writing. From January to February, 1819, he was engaged on what he termed *'a little poem'*—'The Eve of St Agnes'. This, Keats told George and Georgiana in his letter of 14 February, was written while he was at Chichester, visiting relatives of Charles Dilke. Between February and June, 1819, was a period of tremendous creative energy, when he produced 'The Eve of St Mark', 'La Belle Dame sans Merci', and all the famous odes, except 'To Autumn'. It seemed he was within reach of his ambition of being *'among the English Poets'*.

But his writing was not achieved against an untroubled background. His poetry was created in spite of—perhaps even because of—extreme tensions and anxieties in his personal life. A major problem was his growing attachment to Fanny Brawne. At this time Charles Dilke and his wife had decided to move to the Westminster area, and the Brawne family, having been pleased with Wentworth Place during their summer stay, were to move into the Dilkes' half. This meant that Keats, living in the other half of the house with Brown, would be thrown into unavoidable contact with Fanny, without the financial stability, necessary in the social climate of the day, to proceed further with his courtship.

A further nagging worry was his sore throat, which, he told his sister Fanny in February, *'has haunted me at intervals nearly a twelve-month'.*[29] It was only a few months since he had seen Tom die, and with his family background of death from tuberculosis, the sore throat must indeed have seemed ominous.

Money troubles were an ever-present worry; and he even toyed with the idea of becoming a ship's surgeon on an Indiaman. But this plan was abandoned when he decided to revisit the Isle of Wight with a sick friend, Rice.

Some sort of understanding had been reached by this time with Fanny Brawne, to whom Keats wrote from Shanklin. But his passion for her caused him pain as well as pleasure, as may be judged both by the terms in which he addresses her—

> *Ask yourself my love whether you are not very cruel to have so entrammelled me, so destroyed my freedom—*[30]

and by the fact that he was in the process of writing 'Lamia', where the beautiful girl who promises the pleasures of love to Lycius is, in reality, a serpent.

Simultaneously with 'Lamia', he was writing *Otho the Great*, his first excursion into the world of drama. At the end of July, Brown joined Keats in Shanklin, and Rice left; Brown and Keats then worked together on *Otho*, but moved to Winchester in mid-August *'for the convenience of a library'*.

Keats' personal affairs continued to be depressing. His letters to Fanny show emotional turmoil, and are very far from conventional declarations of love; at the end of July, 1819, he wrote:

> *I have two luxuries to brood over in my walks, your Loveliness and the hour of my death. O that I could have possession of them both in the same minute.*[31]

His need to make money to enable them to marry seemed a nightmare; he had never troubled about such things—*'I am as entirely above all matters of interest as the Sun is above the Earth'*[32] he declared. The idea that his love for Fanny might force him, of financial necessity, into writing to please the popular taste, was a very bitter thought. He wrote in disgust to John Taylor, his publisher:

> *I equally dislike the favour of the public with the love of a woman—they are both a cloying treacle to the wings of independence.*[33]

In the midst of these problems, he received a letter containing *'not the best news'*[34] from George, who was also in financial difficulty. It is a measure of his generosity that in his reply, far from blaming George, he assures him, *'You have done your best—Take matters as coolly as you can.'* He will send George what money he can:

> *Your wants will be a fresh spur to me. I assure you you will more than share what I can get.*[35]

The weight of responsibility was pressing hard on Keats. He was, after all, not yet twenty-four; he had nursed a young brother until death, felt keenly that he was *'the only Protector'* of his sister Fanny —and at the same time felt the hopelessness of his own love affair. A reunion with Fanny Brawne in early October, when he immediately declared himself *'dazzled'* by her, offered only a brief respite. At the beginning of 1820, George arrived for a short visit to England in an endeavour to sort out his affairs—an endeavour which created further financial problems for Keats.

Then, in early February, 1820, came the beginning of the end; he coughed up blood, and he knew he would die.

From this time onward, the tone of his letters indicates his acceptance of imminent death. In a letter to James Rice on 14 February, 1820, he writes:

> *How astonishingly does the chance of leaving the world impress a sense of its natural beauties on us. Like poor Falstaff, though I do not babble, I think of green fields.*[36]

To Fanny he confided his thought that, *'If I should die, I have left no immortal work behind me.'*

However, death did not come at once. He gradually recuperated, and by March he was feeling much better except for *'want of strength and a little tightness in the chest'*.[37] Then, in June, he suffered *'a slight spitting of blood . . . which returned rather more copiously at night'*,[38] and began to think of a stay in Italy. His position seemed hopeless, and his feelings for Fanny vacillated between desire, jealousy, bitterness and despair.

> *I should like to give up the matter at once—I should like to die*[39]

he wrote to her in August, adding:

> *I am sickened at the brute world which you are smiling with. I hate men and women more.*[40]

As news spread of Keats' illness, and his need to winter abroad, he received an invitation from Shelley, whom he had met at Leigh Hunt's house, to stay with him in Pisa. It was an invitation Keats

3. *John Keats* by J. Severn, 1821. John Keats in the year of his death—a miniature painted by his friend, Severn, who nursed him throughout his last illness in Rome. (National Portrait Gallery, London)

did not take up, but plans were made for him to go to Rome, under the care of a Dr Clark. It was arranged that Keats' travelling companion was to be his artist friend, Joseph Severn. They were to set sail for Naples, and then travel on to Rome.

After a difficult crossing, their ship arrived in the Bay of Naples in October, 1820, only to find that quarantine regulations meant

they were confined on board for ten days, being finally released on 31 October. His passion for Fanny was a perpetual agony to Keats, and he wrote in anguish to Brown of his torment. *'Where can I look for consolation or ease?'* he asked. *'If I had any chance of recovery, this passion would kill me.'*[41]
But he had no chance of recovery. From mid-November, when he arrived in Rome, Keats was devotedly nursed by Severn and Dr Clark. Further violent haemorrhages occurred in December, however, and it was obvious that he could not last much longer. He grew rapidly weaker, and died in the evening of 23 February, 1821. He was buried in the Protestant Cemetery at Rome, and the epitaph on his tombstone, at his own request, reads:

Here lies one whose name was writ in water.

[1] 'Sleep and Poetry' 96–8 [2] Hugh I'Anson Fausset (ed.) *Letters of John Keats* (Nelson, 1938) pp. 32–3 (All extracts from Keats' letters are taken from this collection, and will subsequently be identified by the initials, K.L.) [3] K.L. p. 35 [4] K.L. p. 64 [5] K.L. p. 69 [6] K.L. pp. 100–101 [7] K.L. p. 135 [8] K.L. p. 137 [9] 'Isabella, or the Pot of Basil' XIV, 3–4; XV, 5–8 [10] K.L. p. 129 [11] K.L. p. 139 [12] K.L. p. 151 [13] K.L. pp. 151–2 [14] K.L. p. 225 [15] K.L. p. 158 [16] K.L. p. 159 [17] K.L. p. 164 [18] K.L. p. 173 [19] K.L. p. 179 [20] K.L. p. 191 [21] K.L. p. 195 [22] K.L. p. 195 [23] K.L. p. 205 [24] K.L. p. 214 [25] K.L. p. 226 [26] K.L. p. 242 [27] K.L. p. 245 [28] K.L. p. 252 [29] K.L. p. 255 [30] K.L. p. 289 [31] K.L. p. 303 [32] K.L. p. 313 [33] K.L. p. 316 [34] K.L. p. 327 [35] K.L. p. 333 [36] K.L. p. 365 [37] K.L. p. 382 [38] K.L. p. 393 [39] K.L. p. 402 [40] K.L. p. 402 [41] K.L. p. 416

2

Towards a Biography of Shelley

Percy Bysshe Shelley was born on 4 August, 1792, at Field Place in Sussex. He seemed predestined to a life of upper-class ease amidst the best of English society. His father, Timothy Shelley, was heir to Sir Bysshe Shelley, and Percy Bysshe was the eldest child, and heir, to Timothy; his path in life appeared clear and fortunate.

But from the start, Shelley refused to fit into the niche which life had provided for him. He astonished his parents by wild escapades —or by accounts of escapades which had never really happened. His friend, the novelist Thomas Love Peacock, writing of this in his *Memoirs of Percy Bysshe Shelley* comments on:

> the habit, thus early developed in Shelley, of narrating, as real, events which had never occurred.

Some of Shelley's boyish whims were less peaceful. One of his four sisters, Hellen, later recalled their *'terror'* when:

> my brother commenced his studies in chemistry, and practised electricity upon us. . . . Whenever he came to me with his piece of folded brown packing-paper under his arm and a bit of wire and a bottle . . . my heart would sink.[1]

If Shelley was unconventional in his behaviour at home, he was equally so at school. Sent to Syon House Academy at the age of ten, he was unhappy and isolated, and found consolation only in his holiday experiments with gunpowder and electricity. Later, he was sent to Eton, where he was even more wretched, and again it was his refusal to conform which lay at the root of his misery. *'Refusing to fag at Eton'*, wrote Mary Shelley in later years:

> he was treated with revolting cruelty by masters and boys: this roused instead of taming his spirit, and he rejected the duty of obedience when it was enforced by menaces and punishment.

Mary Shelley attributed this to Shelley's *'sense of good and justice'* and *'a determined resistance to oppression'*. She is not necessarily a

4. *Percy Bysshe Shelley* by Amelia Curran, 1819. The unruly hair, glowing eyes and somewhat informal costume idealize Shelley as a 'Romantic', unconventional but ardent. (National Portrait Gallery, London)

biased witness; a certain W. S. Halliday, a contemporary of Shelley's at Eton wrote, in a letter quoted by Peacock:

> *He had great moral courage, and feared nothing but what was base, and false, and low.*

Mary also comments that Shelley was *'Inspired with ardour for the acquisition of knowledge'*, and this view is fully endorsed by Thomas Jefferson Hogg, who met Shelley at Oxford University in 1810. (Forty-five years later, Hogg wrote a biography of Shelley,

Shelley's Family

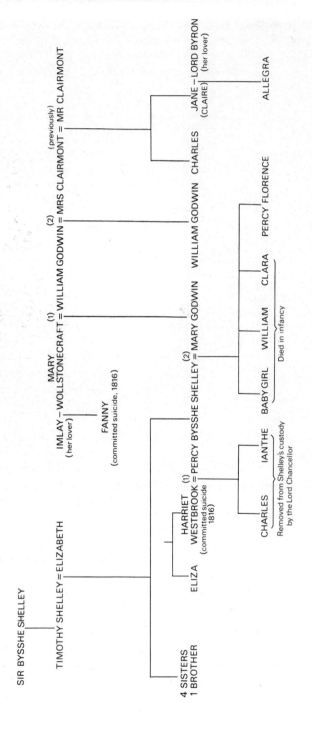

which must rank as a perfect example of 'damning with faint praise'. While referring to Shelley as *'divine'* and *'immortal'*, Hogg manages to paint a picture of their relationship in which Hogg, if anyone, emerges as the hero.) In spite of his many denigrating comments, Hogg admits that he was impressed by Shelley's:

> *zealous earnestness for the augmentation of knowledge, and the glowing philanthropy and boundless benevolence . . .*

He also came face to face with Shelley's passionate love of science; the poet talked till the early hours of:

> *the wonders of chemistry . . . asserting that chemistry was, in truth, the only science that deserved to be studied,*

and when Hogg visited Shelley's room he found it littered with dozens of items amongst which could be discerned:

> *an electrical machine, an air-pump, the galvanic trough, a solar microscope, and large glass jars and receivers.*

However, Hogg admits that he felt only *'slight interest in the subject of the conversation'*, and so had leisure to observe his new acquaintance whom he then describes:

> *His figure was slight and fragile, and yet his bones and joints were large and strong. He was tall, but he stooped so much that he seemed of a low stature. His clothes were expensive, and made according to the most approved mode of the day; but they were tumbled, rumpled, unbrushed. His gestures were abrupt, and sometimes violent, occasionally even awkward, yet more frequently gentle and graceful. His complexion was delicate and almost feminine, of the purest red and white; yet he was tanned and freckled by exposure to the sun. . . . His features, his whole face, and particularly his head, were in fact, unusually small; yet the last appeared of a remarkable bulk, for his hair was long and bushy.*

Hogg goes on to comment on his intelligence, his beautiful *'moral expression'* and his *'air of profound religious veneration'*, but with a quick swoop from the sublime to the ridiculous adds that he felt he would never be able to endure the society of this paragon, because of Shelley's voice. It was, he tells us:

> *intolerably shrill, harsh and discordant; of the most cruel intension—it was perpetual and without any remission—it excoriated the ears.*

However, Hogg somehow managed to overcome the *'excoriation'*, and they remained close friends. They began to work together on a pamphlet entitled *The Necessity of Atheism*, which Shelley then circulated—an act of recklessness in an institution run largely by clergymen. The pamphlet was issued anonymously, but Shelley and Hogg were challenged with being its authors. They both denied the charge, but were nevertheless sent down.

Timothy Shelley was horrified at this new evidence that his son refused to conform to the standards and decencies of society. On his part, whereas Hogg eventually returned to his parents, Percy Bysshe Shelley refused to go home, and found lodgings in London. Shelley's father came to see him, but the visit resulted only in further arguments and mutual bitterness. In fact, Shelley had mistrusted his father for years, for, as Peacock tells us, Shelley had a continual fear that his father wanted him locked up as a madman. This may well have been quite false, says Peacock, but adds:

> *However this may have been, the idea that his father was continually on the watch for a pretext to lock him up, haunted him through life.*

So Shelley remained in London, and occupied much of his time by furthering his acquaintance with the Westbrook family. The younger daughter, Harriet, had been a schoolfellow of Shelley's sisters, Elizabeth and Hellen. In May, 1811, Shelley wrote to Hogg informing him that, *'I spend most of my time at Miss Westbrook's.'* There were two sisters, but it was the sixteen-year-old Harriet whom Shelley came to admire, calling her *'most noble, yet not so cultivated as the elder—a larger diamond, yet not so highly polished'*.

Then a brief reconciliation took place between Shelley and his family, and he returned to Field Place in mid-May, 1811. He went on to stay with his cousin at Rhyader in Radnorshire, but he had by no means forgotten the Westbrook family. Indeed he was not allowed to forget them, for he suddenly received a letter containing a direct appeal from Harriet to save her. He wrote to Hogg:

> *Her father has persecuted her in a most horrible way, by endeavouring to compel her to go to school. She asked my advice: resistance was the answer. . . . And in consequence of my advice she has thrown herself upon my protection.*

Shelley commented to Hogg that it was flattering to be so distinguished by a young lady, and that *'Gratitude and admiration'* demanded that he should love her for ever. He laid his plans accordingly, and Hogg suddenly received a note instructing him to:

> *Direct to the Edinburgh Post Office—my own name. I passed tonight with the mail. Harriet is with me. We are in a slight pecuniary distress.*

Joining them in Edinburgh, Hogg found that they were married; Shelley was not quite nineteen, and Harriet was sixteen.

The marriage caused various immediate problems, one of which was that Shelley had made no secret of his opposition to matrimony on principle. He had upheld this view strongly in conversations with an intellectual friend, a Miss Elizabeth Hitchener; consequently, writing from York in October, 1811, he tried to justify his action, explaining that it was useless to be ostracized by society for making a lone stand:

> *until reasoning has made so comprehensive a change as to emancipate the experimentalist from the resulting evils, and the prejudice with which his opinion . . . would be heard by the immense majority.*[2]

It was an attitude which made sound common sense, but which Shelley was less and less able to adopt; from now on he became more of an *'experimentalist'*, and the *'resulting evils'* isolated him still further from society.

Another immediate result of the marriage was the fury of Shelley's father, who wrote to Hogg's father about it, ending miserably: *'God only knows what can be the end of all this disobedience.'*

Shelley and Harriet, with the faithful Hogg, who had shared their honeymoon and was still with them, travelled south to York. There, arrangements were made for Harriet's sister, Eliza, to join them. Hogg sarcastically calls her *'the peerless Eliza'*; he expected someone:

> *exquisitely beautiful; an elegant figure, full of grace . . . dark, bright eyes, jet black hair, glossy,*

but in reality:

> *The lovely face was seamed with the smallpox, and of a dead white . . . as white, indeed, as a mass of boiled rice, but of a dingy hue, like rice boiled in dirty water.*

Hogg's account is vicious; but Peacock relates how Shelley also hated Eliza, revealing his feelings to Peacock after Harriet's death. It seems likely that Eliza's arrival was the beginning of the end of the marriage.

A further cause of dissension was Hogg himself. Writing to Elizabeth Hitchener in October, 1811, Shelley asserts:

> *My friend Hogg and myself consider our property as common.*[3]

However, when Shelley discovered that Hogg's views on communal property extended to Harriet, he was horrified:

> *Can you conceive that he would have attempted to* seduce my wife?[4]

and he described Hogg as *'the meanest slave of the most contemptible prejudices.'*

Hogg was therefore left behind while Shelley, Harriet and Eliza moved down to the Lake District, to Keswick. There, Shelley met the poet Southey, brother-in-law of Samuel Taylor Coleridge. Shelley had admired Southey's early idealism, but he was soon to become disillusioned by what he saw as Southey's rejection of liberalism for conservative principles. At this stage, however, Shelley found he liked Southey's company, even though:

> *he was not so much a man as a living commonplace book, a talking album filled with long extracts from long-forgotten authors on unimportant subjects.*[5]

Meanwhile Shelley continued to correspond with Elizabeth Hitchener, and urged her to *'come now'* to join them; she would be his *'dearest friend'*, and every thought would be shared with her. Harriet might be his wife, but Elizabeth was *'the sister of* [his] *soul'*.

In a further search for intellectual satisfaction, Shelley took a decision in January, 1812, which was to have profound repercussions on the rest of his life, and to affect him emotionally, socially and financially. He wrote to William Godwin. Godwin was a philosopher who believed that men could live in peace and equality without having laws dictated from above; with his experience of, as he saw it, tyranny and oppression at home, school, and university, this was a view very likely to appeal to Shelley.

Shelley wrote to introduce himself to Godwin, informing the philosopher somewhat ingenuously that he had believed him to be among *'the honourable dead'*. Of himself, Shelley stated—adding hastily, *'Do not suppose that this is vanity'*—*'I am young, I am ardent in the cause of philanthropy and truth.'* He went on to assure Godwin of his *'desire for universal happiness'* and ask for a reply to his letter.

Godwin replied very promptly, but complained that the letter was too generalized. Shelley obliged by giving more particulars about himself—including the information that he was *'heir by entail to an estate of £6,000 per annum'*, a piece of information to which Godwin was by no means indifferent, as became apparent in years to come when he frequently demanded, and received, sums of money from Shelley.

Meanwhile, however, Shelley had decided to move to Ireland. Keswick was probably proving rather trying; Shelley had already fallen foul of the *'strange prejudices'* of *'these country people'* the previous November when explaining the nature of the atmosphere to Harriet and Eliza:

> *and, to illustrate my theory, I made some experiments on hydrogen gas, one of its constituent parts. This was in the garden, and the vivid flame was seen at some distance.*[6]

The landlord had complained, and, although Shelley managed to placate him, was *'by no means certain'* that he would let them remain.

But a far more positive reason for removing from Keswick to Ireland was the political campaign which Shelley intended to mount from Dublin. Writing to Godwin at the end of January, 1812, Shelley explains that he has been *'preparing an address to the Catholics of Ireland'* and that he will devote himself:

> *with unremitting zeal, as far as uncertain state of health will permit, towards forwarding the great ends of virtue and happiness in Ireland.*[7]

Accordingly, Harriet, Eliza and Shelley made the sea-crossing, arriving in Dublin in February, 1812, and Shelley began to circulate his pamphlet. Hogg dismisses the *Address to the Irish People* as *'poorly and feebly written'* but it must have seemed fiery stuff to the Irish in 1812, reading Shelley's pronouncements that:

> *The goodness of a government consists in the happiness of the governed,*

and that:

> *the superfluities taken from the rich would be sufficient when spread abroad to make everyone comfortable.*

Shelley himself was certainly deeply moved by the plight of the Irish. Writing to Godwin, with whom he now maintained an extensive correspondence, he admits:

> *I had no conception of the depth of human misery until now. The poor of Dublin are assuredly the meanest and most*

> *miserable of all. In their narrow streets thousands seem huddled together—one mass of animate filth.*[8]

(It is interesting to note that it was the Irish poor, too, who had most forcibly struck Keats with their wretchedness when he and Brown paid a quick visit from Scotland; the description of the *'Duchess of Dunghill'*, quoted in Chapter 7, was the result.)

Godwin wrote to warn Shelley that he was *'preparing a scene of blood'* by rousing the Irish, but Shelley refused to see it in this light; and, to do him justice, his pamphlet repeatedly stressed the evils of violence and the need to:

> *forward the cause of reform . . . by employing your leisure time in reasoning or the cultivation of your minds.*

However, the campaign in Ireland was soon over, and by April Shelley was writing to Godwin from Nantgwilt in Wales. He was not finding life easy. He and his *ménage* had *'traversed the whole of North and part of South Wales'* looking for a house to lease. They were now temporarily settled and wished to stay, as:

> *The cheapness, beauty and retirement make this place in every point of view desirable,*[9]

but were *'not yet completely certain of being able to obtain the house'*. And indeed, by June, Shelley wrote again sadly, *'We are unexpectedly compelled to quit Nantgwilt.'* Once again the Shelley family were on their travels.

This time they went south, to Lynmouth in Devon, and settled into a cottage, with small rooms, but, as Shelley wrote, *'the poverty and humbleness of the apartments is compensated by their number.'* From here, he wrote urging Godwin to let his stepdaughter Fanny join them. He was also hoping that Elizabeth Hitchener would come —she was *'about to become an inmate of our family'*—and that a kind of Shelley commune would be set up. Godwin, too, was not excluded: *'Come, thou venerated and excellent friend,'* Shelley urged. The venerated and excellent friend finally accepted the invitation, and arrived at Lynmouth, only to find that Shelley, Miss Hitchener, who had at last joined the group, Harriet, and Eliza had once more set off on their travels, and no one knew where they had gone.

In fact, Shelley and his three ladies had moved in a hurry, for their servant had been caught distributing Shelley's political tracts. It became expedient to leave the area at once, and so yet again they sought a home in Wales.

Paying a visit to London, with Harriet, Eliza and Elizabeth Hitchener, in October, 1812, Shelley called on Hogg, whom he had not seen for a year, and told him of his latest scheme. He was living at Tremadoc, and was very keen to support a plan whereby:

> *Some four or five thousand acres of fertile land were to be gained from the sea*[10]

by building a sea-wall. It was just the sort of scheme to appeal to Shelley—practical, with obvious beneficial effects to the local people. But although Shelley tried, he could not rouse much enthusiasm in the people of Sussex, and described them as *'a parcel of cold, selfish, and calculating animals'*. For himself, however:

> *my fervid hopes, my ardent desires, my unremitting personal exertions (as far as my health will allow) are all engaged in that cause, which I will desert* but with my life.[11]

5. *William Godwin* by K. W. Pickersgill. Godwin, Mary Shelley's father, corresponded frequently with the young poet, but opposed his marriage to Mary. (National Portrait Gallery, London)

While in London, Shelley took the opportunity of visiting God-win, and in spite of the philosopher's unfortunate visit to Lyn-mouth, they were delighted with each other. Godwin had been married to Mary Wollstonecraft, and after her death had remarried a Mrs Clairmont. His somewhat mixed family consisted of Charles and Jane Clairmont, Mrs Godwin's children by her previous marriage; Fanny, the child of Mary Wollstonecraft by her lover Imlay; Mary Godwin, the child of Mary Wollstonecraft and God-win; and William Godwin, the son of Godwin and his second wife. During this autumn, however, when Shelley and Harriet were visiting the Godwins, Jane and Mary were away from home, and it is unlikely that Shelley met Mary, who was to change his life so completely.

Before going back to Wales, the Shelley household diminished; Miss Hitchener left. The ardour which the *'sister of* [his] *soul'* had inspired in Shelley had faded, and it would be surprising if Harriet had not felt some jealousy of the woman to whom her husband had written, *'Henceforth will I be yours—yours with truth, sincerity, and unreserve.'* It was not an amicable parting, but it was certainly a cause for relief to Shelley.

Returning to Wales, Shelley was occupied in writing the poem 'Queen Mab', which describes the present misery of the world, especially the evils of monarchy, and the glorious day of liberty which must come. It was not in itself to be a particularly didactic poem, but the notes to it were to be *'long and philosophical'.*

The disillusionment with the world expressed in the poem was now extending itself to the Tremadoc venture, *'in which I thought-lessly engaged'*, as Shelley wrote to Hogg. The final blow came at the end of February, 1813, when, as Harriet wrote to tell their friend, Thomas Hookham, their house at Tannyrallt was attacked by an armed intruder. When Shelley fired at him, he swore horrible revenge, and returned later to renew the attack, firing through Shelley's *'flannel gown . . . and the window curtain'.* Peacock, visiting Tannyrallt later to look at the evidence, was sceptical that any attack had taken place. Hogg, too, was doubtful: *'I never met with any person who believed in it,'* he wrote. However, it seems certain that something genuinely frightened the Shelleys. Harriet, who was expecting her first child, was only too happy to leave; she was con-vinced that it was a plot to drive them out, because of Shelley's political pamphleteering. *'Everyone seemed to be plotting against us,'* she complained.

So they moved again—this time back to Dublin, and thence to

Western Ireland. Hogg travelled to Dublin to see them, but they were already in Killarney; Harriet and Shelley arrived back in Dublin the day after he left, and followed him to London. There, in June, 1813, shortly before Shelley's twenty-first birthday, Harriet's baby, Eliza Ianthe, was born.

Shelley was optimistic that, when he reached his majority, he would have greater financial freedom and was depressed to discover that his family intended to take legal action to block his inheritance. As ever, travel seemed a source of relief, and so Shelley, Harriet, Eliza (inevitably), baby Ianthe, and their friend Peacock travelled north, to the Lake District, and on to Edinburgh. But the trip was not a successful one, and by the end of the year they were back in London; shortly afterwards Shelley leased a house in Windsor, and Eliza, of whom he wrote, '*I certainly hate her with all my heart and soul*', went too.

The marriage was rapidly deteriorating, but was, as yet, by no means over. In fact, in March, 1814, Shelley went through a second marriage ceremony with Harriet in case of legal difficulties over the Scottish marriage. Yet, in the following months, Harriet and Shelley were frequently apart, and it seemed as if a final separation was inevitable. Then, in late May or early June, Shelley met Godwin's daughter, Mary, and fell in love with her.

Thomas Love Peacock, in his memoirs of Shelley, insists that Mary was the sole cause of the breakup of Shelley's marriage to Harriet:

> *There was no estrangement, no shadow of a thought of separation, till Shelley became acquainted . . . with the lady who was subsequently his second wife.*

This seems doubtful, but, whatever the truth of the matter, Peacock is forced to concede the fitness of the match.

> *That Shelley's second wife was intellectually better suited to him than his first, no one who knew them both will deny; and that a man, who lived so totally out of the ordinary world and in a world of ideas, needed such an ever-present sympathy more than the general run of men, must also be admitted.*

Godwin, however, would admit no such thing, and was horrified by the relationship. Harriet, too, returned to London wishing to be reconciled to her husband, for she found that she was expecting his child.

But Shelley did what he always did when in difficulty; he set out on his travels. This time, however, there was a difference. When he set sail for France on 28 July, 1814, it was not Harriet and the ubiquitous Eliza who went with him, but his new love, Mary Godwin, and her step-sister, Jane Clairmont.

6. *Mary Wollstonecraft Shelley* by R. Rothwell, 1841. Although this was painted many years after Shelley's death, it is easy to see in these beautiful, intelligent features what attracted the poet to desert his first wife. (National Portrait Gallery, London)

By mid-September the travellers had returned, after journeying through France to Lucerne. They were met with problems of every kind. The question of Harriet, pregnant and miserable, had to be considered, and financial worries were very pressing. And Mary was also expecting a child.

Then in January, 1815, an event occurred which at first sight seemed of immediate benefit to Shelley. His grandfather, Sir Bysshe, died, and Shelley's father became the new baronet. Shelley moved into the position of heir to the property. However, by the terms of his grandfather's will, Shelley was presented with a difficult choice, the effect of which was that he would only benefit greatly from the estates if he consented to their being entailed. But Shelley's need was for immediate financial aid, not the promise of distant prosperity and it seemed as if his hopes had been falsely raised; however, negotiations with his father eventually produced a respectable income, so that by midsummer, 1815, the financial worries were less pressing.

But Shelley's troubles were by no means over. In February, 1815, Mary gave birth to a premature baby girl; it died within a fortnight.

During the next few months Shelley gradually put his mind to the problem of a place to live, and in August, 1815, they leased a house on the edge of Windsor Park. Shelley now wrote 'Alastor', in which he celebrates the blessings of human love, sought but not found by the dreamer of the poem.

By the beginning of 1816, life seemed far more settled for Shelley and Mary. On 24 January she gave birth to a son, William, who was to be the darling of his parents for a few years.

Meanwhile Jane Clairmont—who now preferred to call herself Clara or Claire, and who had recently been away from the Shelleys, staying in the south of England—returned to London, and, it appears, introduced herself to Lord Byron. Byron was already famous, and infamous, and to begin an affair with such a dashing hero must have seemed an irresistible chance. Byron left England permanently in April, 1816, but Claire was undaunted; Shelley, Mary and baby William had also decided to go abroad and Claire went with them. In May, when Shelley and his party were staying in Geneva, Byron arrived at the same hotel, and the two poets became acquainted. They moved into adjacent residences, and the two relationships—that of Byron with Shelley, and that of Byron with Claire—both flourished in their different ways. It was a fruitful time for both Mary and Claire; the latter found she was expecting Byron's child, while Mary began, for her own amusement, the novel which was to make her instantly famous—*Frankenstein*. It was appropriate that while horror stories were in their minds they should now meet Matthew Gregory Lewis, the writer whose tale of Gothic horror, *The Monk*, had given him a reputation both for talent and for impropriety; he was the guest of Lord Byron, who had a similar reputation.

In September, Shelley, Mary, Claire, the baby and his Swiss nurse, all returned to England. Shelley left the others in Bath while he looked for somewhere to live, as the lease on their previous house had expired. Meanwhile, the secret of Claire's relationship with Byron was to be kept from Godwin.

But Godwin had greater griefs to contend with. In October, 1816, Fanny, the daughter of his beloved first wife, the half-sister of his daughter Mary, feeling that her life was useless and a burden to others, travelled to Bristol, took a room in an inn and committed suicide. A month later, news arrived that Shelley's wife, Harriet, had drowned herself.

Shelley immediately tried to claim custody of his two children by Harriet, Ianthe and Charles. He also decided to do what he was formerly not free to do—marry Mary. The marriage to Mary was performed before the end of the year, but Shelley was never able to obtain custody of Harriet's children, and it was a bitter blow. Writing in his memoirs, Peacock tells us that:

> the judgement . . . rests entirely on moral conduct. It was distinctly laid down that the principles which Shelley had professed in regard to some of the most important relations of life, had been carried by him into practice.

The decision, made by the Lord Chancellor, Eldon, was one which Shelley never forgave.

Meanwhile, in January, 1817, Claire Clairmont gave birth to Lord Byron's daughter, and called her Alba. Later, at Byron's request, she was to be known as Allegra, and was to be the innocent cause of much misery to her mother and Shelley.

But these were not all gloomy times. In his younger days, Shelley had written to introduce himself to the writer and publisher Leigh Hunt, in much the same way that he had later written to Godwin. In December, 1816, they had met, and been pleased with each other's company. Now, in February, 1817, they renewed the acquaintance, and, at Hunt's house in Hampstead, Shelley was to meet two other young poets—Keats and Reynolds.

At this time, Keats was involved with his first long poem, 'Endymion'. Shelley also embarked on a major work, 'Laon and Cythna', later to be published as 'The Revolt of Islam'. This, like his prose works of this year—*Putting Reform to the Vote* and *On the Death of the Princess Charlotte*—was political propaganda, urging liberty and justice for all.

Towards the end of 1817, Shelley's recurrent bouts of ill-health grew worse, and he was once again thinking of going abroad. By early 1818 it was decided that the Shelley family should go to Italy, and in March he left England—for ever, as it transpired. Mary, her son William, her baby Clara, born in September, 1817, and Claire Clairmont with Allegra, went with him, and they settled in Milan, from where Claire and Shelley both wrote to Lord Byron about his daughter. He was prepared to look after her and acknowledge her, but Claire must give her up absolutely. Shelley knew Claire's misery over this, and tried to intercede; but the final arrangements were made, and in April, 1818, Allegra travelled with her nurse to Venice. In the event, Claire's unhappiness over parting with her daughter was well-founded, for four years later the child was dead, having been kept, at the end, hidden from her mother in a convent.

Shelley, Mary and Claire settled at Livorno, and there Shelley immersed himself in work. He translated Plato's *Symposium*, and later began thinking of *Prometheus Unbound*. But it seemed that they were never to be free from grief. In September, 1818, baby Clara grew suddenly ill and was dead within a few days.

Again travel was decided upon as a source of relief. This time they went south, to Rome first, and on to Naples. Rome amazed Shelley. *'The impression of it'*, he wrote to Peacock,

> *exceeds anything I have ever experienced in my travels. . . . The Coliseum is unlike any work of human hands I ever saw before. . . . But a small part of the exterior circumference remains—it is exquisitely light and beautiful.*[12]

Naples, too, impressed them, especially their excursion to Vesuvius, and it was there that he completed the first act of *Prometheus Unbound*.

After Naples, they returned to Rome, where Shelley wrote the next two acts of *Prometheus*. Mary was now expecting a baby in the autumn of 1819, and all seemed to be going well. Then the most bitter blow fell: their most precious and only surviving child, William, died on 7 June.

The tragedy which was only too close to him at this time is reflected in the work which Shelley produced during this summer. On their arrival in Rome, Shelley had become interested in the story of the violent lives and deaths of the Cenci family, and decided to write a drama. In spite of the loss of William, or perhaps because of it, he worked on, and by August the play was finished. By this time, they had returned to Livorno, where Shelley received news of the Massacre of Peterloo. At a mass meeting in support of constitutional reform, held on St Peter's Field, Manchester, the crowd had been dispersed by sabre-wielding cavalry; eleven of them had died and four hundred were injured. Shelley's reply was the bitter poem 'The Mask of Anarchy'. Thinking, perhaps, of the withholding of Charles and Ianthe, and the deaths of his three children by Mary, Shelley wrote:

> Next came Fraud, and he had on
> Like Eldon, an ermined gown.
> His big tears, for he wept well,
> Turned to mill-stones as they fell.
>
> And the little children, who
> Round his feet played to and fro
> Thinking every tear a gem
> Had their brains knocked out by them.[13]

In the autumn, the Shelleys moved to Florence, and there, in November, 1819, their only surviving child was born—Percy, also given the name Florence, who was to survive his father and his half-brother Charles, and to inherit the baronetcy.

Political questions still occupied Shelley's mind. He was now writing perhaps his deepest political pamphlet, *A Philosophical View of Reform*, which sums up all his political campaigning of the previous eight years. His view of reform is epitomized by his assertion that:

> The broad principle of political reform is the natural equality of men, not with relation to their property but to their rights.

Shelley was not too deeply engrossed in his own work and personal worries to ignore others' problems. He had heard of the illness of Keats, and in July, 1820, wrote urging him to come to stay with Mary and himself at Pisa, where they had now taken up residence. The offer was never accepted, and in fact Shelley himself suffered from increasingly poor health. Early in 1821, Shelley heard that Keats had died at Rome, and the fine, moving lament of 'Adonais' was written in his memory.

During the early months of 1821, the Shelleys were widening their circle of acquaintances in Pisa. Two of their new friends were Edward and Jane Williams, and they soon became very close. Meanwhile, new literary schemes were afoot. In the autumn of 1821, Byron came with his entourage to Pisa, and a scheme was devised whereby, as Shelley wrote to Leigh Hunt, Byron proposed that Hunt:

should come and go shares with him and me in a periodical work, to be conducted here; in which each of the contracting parties should publish all their original composition and share the profits.[14]

Another new acquaintance of this period was Edward John Trelawny, a wanderer and adventurer by inclination and by profession. Edward Williams, Trelawny, Shelley and Byron all discovered a delight in sailing, and planned to spend the coming summer at the boating centre of La Spezia. Trelawny produced plans, and he, Shelley and Williams decided to have a boat built for them, which was to be called the *Don Juan*. Byron had his own yacht, the *Bolivar*. In pursuance of their scheme of sailing, the Shelleys hired for the summer of 1822 the Casa Magni, a house in a cove on the bay of La Spezia. Sharing the house were Edward and Jane Williams and— returned from Florence, where she had been acting as a governess —Claire Clairmont.

Once again, however, the Shelleys were to find private grief broke upon them. It was at Casa Magni, in early May, that Claire heard of the death of her beloved Allegra. And in June Mary suffered a violent miscarriage, and nearly died.

It must have seemed a joyful piece of news when, a few days later, they heard that Leigh Hunt and his wife and children had reached Genoa after a difficult and lengthy voyage. Hunt had come to Italy to escape persecution and to join Shelley and Byron in their scheme for a periodical. On the first of July, Shelley heard that the Hunts were setting out from Genoa, and he and Williams set out for Livorno. They met the Hunts and Shelley escorted them to Pisa. Returning to Livorno, he found Williams eager to return home. With a cabin boy on board, they set sail for Casa Magni, but never arrived. Some days later, their bodies were washed ashore.

When Shelley's ashes were later buried in Rome, they were, Trelawny tells us:

covered . . . with solid stone, inscribed with a Latin epitaph written by Leigh Hunt.

Perhaps a better, though longer epitaph, is his friend Peacock's summary of his poetic ability:

 a genius unsurpassed in the description and imagination of scenes of beauty and grandeur; in the expression of impassioned love of ideal beauty; in the illustration of deep feeling by congenial imagery, and in the infinite variety of harmonious versification. What was, in my opinion, deficient in his poetry was . . . the want of reality in the characters with which he addressed or imparted the utterance of his impassioned feelings. He was advancing, I think, to the attainment of this reality. It would have given to his poetry the only element of truth which it wanted; though at the same time, the more clear development of what men were would have lowered his estimate of what they might be, and dimmed his enthusiastic prospect of the future destiny of the world.

[1] T. J. Hogg *The Life of Shelley* in *The Life of Percy Bysshe Shelley* (2 vols)(Dent, 1933) p. 23   [2] R. B. Johnson (ed.) *Letters of Shelley* (Bodley Head, 1929) p. 53   [3] *ibid.* pp. 57–8   [4] *ibid.* p. 60   [5] as 1, p. 290   [6] as 2, p. 62   [7] as 1, p. 311   [8] *ibid.* p. 326   [9] *ibid.* p. 342   [10] *ibid.* p. 368   [11] *ibid.* p. 369   [12] A S. B. Glover (ed.) *Shelley: Selected Poetry, Prose and Letters* (Nonesuch Press, 1951) p. 1082   [13] 'The Masque of Anarchy' IV–V   [14] as 12, p. 1102

3

The French Revolution: Political Changes

The age in which Keats and Shelley lived—and died, as they both died young—was an age of change, of revolution in both its literal and modern sense. The old values and the established order of life—monarchy, episcopal church, aristocracy, and a carefully structured social order of rank and privilege—were being questioned, threatened, and overturned throughout Europe, and, further afield, in America. The poetry of the age, especially that of Shelley, reflects this sense of upheaval, alteration and re-creation, though many of the most obvious and violent changes had taken place before he was born and well before he began to write.

Throughout the second half of the eighteenth century, the accepted constitutional order in Britain was repeatedly challenged. Radical movements and individual reformers were constantly agitating for a new system of franchise to replace the haphazard and totally unequal system of voting qualifications. The power of the King and his judiciary was challenged by such issues as the arrest of John Wilkes, who, in 1763, published an attack on the King's minister, Bute, in his paper *The North Briton* and was seized on a general warrant—that is, one which mentioned no names. Wilkes took action in the courts to challenge the validity of general warrants, and his appeal was upheld, much to the discomfiture of George III and to the delight of the populace, who cheered Wilkes in the streets. Wilkes and his supporters again challenged the power of the monarch in 1769, when, although in prison, Wilkes was repeatedly elected to Parliament while the King as repeatedly ensured his expulsion by the House of Commons.

Such evidence of growing unrest and a growing desire for liberty at home was reflected in the situation abroad. In 1776 the American colonies declared their independence of Britain, and took up arms to support their right to freedom in a war which lasted from 1776 to 1783 and which resulted in victory for the colonists.

Then in 1789 the struggle for liberty in France erupted in the Revolution which was to change Europe and which, many reformers hoped, would change the world.

To the English radicals, the situation in France seemed an extreme reflection of their own grievances. The French peasants had no political power, but still suffered under burdensome taxation. Real power was in the hands of an élite, while the supposed representatives of the people, the States-General, had not been summoned since 1614. When the States-General met at last in May, 1789, its intransigent attitude towards the demands of Louis XVI, and its formation of a new National Assembly, dedicated to establishing a new Constitution in France, seemed an inspiring example to those in England who had been pressing for constitutional reform.

7. *The Oath of the Horatii* by Jean-Louis David, 1784. This picture of an event in ancient Rome epitomizes the French Republican dedication to a new, nobler state. (The Louvre, Paris)

The French Establishment's reaction in summoning troop reinforcements to Paris and Versailles showed a similar panic to that displayed in England in reaction to Wilkes. And the results were similar—increased popular support for the revolutionaries.

On 14 July, 1789, when the Bastille, an ancient prison in Paris, was attacked by the mob and the prisoners released, this act of liberation was seen then, and has been regarded since, as highly significant and symbolic—though in fact there were only seven prisoners inside to be released—for the attack on the Bastille stood for a successful attack on tyranny.

8. *Liberty Leading the People* by E. Delacroix, 1831. Although this represents a later uprising, Delacroix exactly captures the spirit of determined optimism which characterized the beginning of the French Revolution. (The Louvre, Paris)

Following the attack on the Bastille, the spirit of revolution spread throughout France. The homes and property of many lords were attacked, and local councils, elected by the people, were established. By August, 1789, the National Assembly had abolished all the old methods of taxation and the power of the King was greatly weakened by the Assembly's Declaration of Rights. Then, following an attack on the palace of Versailles in October, 1789, the Royal Family became virtually prisoners in the Tuileries. In a few months the French Revolutionaries had achieved more than the English radicals had been seeking for years.

But it was not only in the area of constitutional reform that the French Revolution seemed to set an example. Republican feelings had been growing in England, and the implicit and actual attack on the monarchy in France was by no means unwelcome in many quarters.

In his *Reflections on the Revolution in France*, published in 1790, the statesman Burke, writing with an Establishment air of authoritarian common sense, stated confidently:

> *In England ... we cherish and cultivate those inbred sentiments which are ... the true supporters of all liberal and manly morals*

... We fear God; we look up with awe to kings; with affection to parliaments; with duty to magistrates; with reverence to priests; and with respect to nobility. Why? Because when such ideas are brought before our minds, it is natural *to be affected.*

And referring to the question of constitutional reform, he asserted:

I shall only say here, in justice to that old-fashioned constitution, under which we have long prospered, that our representation has been found perfectly adequate to all the purposes for which a representation of the people can be desired or devised.

9. *Edmund Burke*, Studio of Reynolds. The statesman, Edmund Burke, after pleading for greater freedom for the American colonists, saw the dangers of too much freedom in the Revolution in France. (National Portrait Gallery, London)

However, the following year, Thomas Paine published his *Rights of Man*, which put forward exactly the opposite viewpoint, and the unprecedented public acclaim with which it was received showed that Burke had misjudged popular feelings. *Rights of Man* was issued as a direct reply to Burke, and in looking at the French situation Paine directed a barely-disguised threat against the British Establishment. He pointed out that:

> *It was not against Louis XVI, but against the despotic principles of the government, that the nation revolted,*

and added pointedly that deep-rooted despotism could only be removed by *'a complete and universal revolution'.* Whereas Burke said that the English *'looked up'* to kings, Paine averred that *'the race of kings are the most insignificant in capacity'*. Whereas Burke said that his countrymen had *'respect'* for nobility, Paine said pithily that:

> *a body of men, holding themselves accountable to nobody, ought not to be trusted by anybody.*

And, while Burke praised our constitution and system of representation, Paine demanded bitterly:

> *Can, then, Mr Burke produce the English Constitution? If he cannot, we may fairly conclude that though it has been so much talked about, no such thing as a constitution exists, or ever did exist, and consequently the people have yet a constitution to form.*

Paine was by no means a lone voice crying in the wilderness. His book was a huge success, and his ideas were widely circulated. It seemed as if support for the French Revolution was almost universal. The mood of liberalism gave new impetus to the radical movement for parliamentary reform urged by a group of young Whigs under Charles James Fox, who declared that the Revolution was the most magnificent event in the history of the world. Reform Societies sprang up all over England and Scotland; and even the Prince Regent endorsed the enthusiasm. Paine's reply to Burke had exactly caught the feeling of the public.

A further reply to Burke was written in the form of *Vindication of the Rights of Man* by a certain Mary Wollstonecraft. It made her name, and roused considerable admiration in William Godwin, the philosopher, whose fierce support of the Revolution made him the spiritual leader of the English pro-revolutionaries. (Mary Wollstonecraft later wrote *Vindication of the Rights of Women*, and this attack on the conventions of her day was also admired by the equally anti-establishment Godwin. They became lovers in 1796, and married in 1797, when she was expecting his child; she died giving birth to his daughter Mary, who later eloped with the young Shelley.)

Godwin's own reply to Burke was not merely a response to the particular situation at the time. His *Enquiry Concerning Political Justice*, published in 1793, set out a complete, ideal system of society, a kind of Utopia in which man would be convinced by reason of the duty of sharing all property according to need. Beginning with his theory that the human mind is formed by its environment, Godwin goes on to assert the *'perfectibility'* of man and of human society. There is an almost irresistible logic in his declaration that:

> *If justice have any meaning, nothing can be more iniquitous, than for one man to possess superfluities, while there is a human being in existence that is not adequately supplied,*

and one might readily accede to his suggestion that:

> *If superfluity were banished, the necessity for the greater part of the manual industry of mankind would be superseded.*

However, the assertions that *'All men love justice'* and that *'Every man is desirous of assisting another'* lead one to feel that Godwin had not fully studied human nature—a feeling which is reinforced when we find him confident that, once marriage is abolished, several men showing a preference for the same woman will all *'enjoy her conversation'* and *'be wise enough to consider the sensual intercourse as a very trivial object'*.

If Godwin's theories seem idealistic, they were interesting enough at the time, with the spirit of revolution in the air, to attract a great many readers in spite of the three guineas charged for the work. Hazlitt, writing in an essay on William Godwin published in *The Spirit of the Age* in 1825, looked back on the philosopher's popular success at the time:

> *he blazed as a sun in the firmament of reputation; no one was more talked of, more looked up to, more sought after, and wherever liberty, truth, justice was the theme, his name was not far off. . . . No work in our time gave such a blow to the philosophical mind of the country.*

Even so, Hazlitt felt that Godwin *'conceived too nobly of his fellows'* and *'raises the standard of morality above the reach of humanity'*, making no allowance for *'the amiable weaknesses of our nature'*.

However, one disciple of Godwin's who saw no disadvantage in the idealism of his view was the young Shelley, who read *Political Justice* at Eton and for whom it became a gospel. Indeed, many of the theories which Shelley later put forward, in his life, his poetry and his pamphlets, are based on Godwin's views in *Political Justice*. The idea of a community sharing work and produce, of the pointlessness of marriage, of non-violent persuasion—all these in Shelley come from Godwin, and, as we have seen (Chapter 2), when Shelley discovered in 1812 that Godwin, whose fame had now receded, was still alive, the news thrilled him. '*The name of Godwin*', he wrote to the man who later became his father-in-law:

> *has been used to excite in me feelings of reverence and admiration. I have been accustomed to consider him a luminary too dazzling for the darkness which surrounds him.*[1]

For Shelley, in 1812, Godwin still represented the new hope of a better world which had been greeted with such enthusiasm at the start of the French Revolution.

But this tidal wave of enthusiasm had soon diminished. In September, 1792, came the first really clear sign to the outside world that the spirit of freedom and justice which the Revolution had seemed to epitomize, might not be unalloyed. The prisons, formerly full of those oppressed by the nobility, were now full of supposed enemies of the Revolution, and over a thousand of these were summarily tried and executed in that period of five days known as the September Massacres, to which Louis XVI himself fell victim.

A further set-back to the English reformers' view of France as defender of liberty was the declaration of war between the two countries in 1793. French nobles who had fled the country, the *émigrés*, had persuaded the King of Prussia and the Emperor of Austria to declare their support for Louis. In 1793, Britain also entered the war, horrified to see that the Revolution appeared to be spreading outside the borders of France.

In fact, the fears of Britain regarding the nature of the Revolution were all too well founded. In France at this time, the spirit of freedom had been replaced by a spirit of terror, and thousands were executed, some being denounced merely for a lack of Revolutionary zeal. Among the victims of this new wave of violence was Marie Antoinette. Within a few months, even the early Revolutionary leaders themselves were being executed, and Robespierre, a passionate and popular Revolutionary from the first days of the uprising, but later responsible for innumerable deaths, was himself guillotined in 1794. The glorious and inspiring surge for liberty, equality and fraternity had turned out to be a source of new tyranny and oppression.

Further evidence that the Revolutionary ideals were fast fading came in 1795 when the new Assembly, the Convention, decided to do away with the idea of universal suffrage so that the Government would be less under the influence of the people of Paris. Two Councils, the Council of Elders, and the Council of Five Hundred, were to govern, but the daily business of running the country was to be conducted by a Directory of five leaders.

It was at this time that there rose to power an able and ambitious young man from a poor Corsican family; his name was Napoleon Bonaparte.

In 1793, he had led a body of troops in the defeat of a royalist uprising in Toulon, and his obvious military ability led to his being given the command of the French army in Italy, and later of a force invading Egypt. Returning victorious in 1799, he found France in political confusion and engineered a *coup d'état* to take power.

To begin with, Napoleon seemed to be totally opposed to the policies of the old regime. He appeared to epitomize the new spirit of France, and his reform of the legal system—the Napoleonic Code—and his improvements in the fields of education and transport seemed to indicate that he was the great leader France had hoped for.

But gradually it became clear that, if there was to be a new system in France, Napoleon wanted supreme power over all its functions. In 1804 he was proclaimed Emperor, albeit with popular support, and he then set about finding himself an Empire to rule, seeing himself as head of a great and powerful dynasty spread across Europe. To support his position he even created his brothers King of Naples and King of Holland. As his power grew, he seemed invincible; but he was finally defeated by an alliance of European states at Waterloo in 1815, and exiled to St Helena, where he died in 1821. France meanwhile returned to a monarchy under the brother of Louis XVI.

Napoleon could have been a perfect hero for radicals such as Shelley. Coming as he did from a poor family, not aided by hereditary rank and privilege but rising by his own talents in support of a popular Revolution, Napoleon seemed at first a superman, a kind of mortal Prometheus. However, once it became obvious that, albeit along with some social reform, he was setting up a new absolute power in France, the dream faded for many of his supporters. Beethoven had intended to dedicate a new symphony to Napoleon as supporter of high ideals of freedom and justice; but the news that Napoleon had accepted the title of Emperor was a bitter

blow to the composer, who entitled his work *Eroica* instead. Similarly Shelley had at first seen Napoleon as *'that most fiery spirit'*,
who would bring freedom to the world; but, in 'Lines Written on
Hearing the News of the Death of Napoleon', Shelley describes him
as *'a torrent of ruin'*; the earth is shrouded in *'his shame . . . the hopes
that from his glory fled'*.

The downfall of Napoleon marked the end of the hopes that had
been aroused at the start of the French Revolution. Disillusionment
replaced optimism. But the disillusionment could not eradicate the
fact that Europe had been in turmoil for twenty-five years, and that
the French Revolution had been an event of world-shaking pro-
portions, which left its mark on Europe for ages to come. The ideal
might not have been achieved; but ideas had been fermented which
were to inspire reformists for decades.

The enthusiasm which the French Revolution had aroused in
young men of the 1790s was recorded by the poet Wordsworth
some years later in his *Prelude*. Those who were *'strong in love'*
exulted in the *'dawn'* of a new era, in the *'pleasant exercise of hope
and joy'* which swept away *'the meagre, stale, forbidding ways of
custom, law and statute'*. He recalled favourable impressions made
by a visit to France in 1791–2. In 1792, the September Massacres
had just taken place; but appalled as he was by them, he felt that a
new democratic leadership was necessary, and had to be forcefully
established. Inspired with an idealistic concept of the Revolution,
he was prepared to admit that some temporary suffering was
necessary in order to establish permanent benefits. To Wordsworth,
and to many of his contemporaries, the French Revolution seemed
at first to be not so much a historical event as a turning-point in
the existence of man, the start of an ideal civilization:

> *we should see the earth
> Unthwarted in her wish o recompense
> The meek, the lowly patient child of toil,*
> *All institutes for ever blotted out
> That legalised execution. . . .
> Should see the people having a strong hand
> In framing their own laws.*[2]

Wordsworth's fond hopes were soon to be disillusioned. As seems
inevitable, rule by the people changed to rule by the few, and then
to rule by one as Napoleon grew to power. Burke was proved right
in his prophecies, and fear of dissent grew stronger in Britain than
revolutionary enthusiasm. John Reeves, a lawyer returning to

England from Canada in 1792, was horrified at the communistic, republican ideas which were abroad, and founded 'An Association for Preserving Liberty and Property against Republicans and Levellers'. The Parliamentary 'Speech from the Throne' in the same year declared that *'a design existed to subvert the constitution'*, and in 1794, several eminent members of the London Reform Group were tried for High Treason. In 1799 the Government passed the harsh Combination Laws, forbidding the association of workmen in societies for the sake of improving conditions or wages. The disillusionment of reality had replaced the wave of idealism.

In England, then, the Revolution, the rise of Napoleon, and his acquisition of power, did more damage than merely disappoint idealists. As the British Government became horrified at the rate with which the French Revolution gained momentum, the first enthusiasm changed to fear and then to repression as the war with France continued. Constitutional reform, which had been gradually gaining headway in British politics, was now seen as a threat to national security, and all reform as the thin end of the revolutionary wedge. A new conservatism entered the British soul.

But radical energies and hopes had been aroused; a belief that a society based on equality, liberty and justice could emerge, had inspired the thinking men of England for years. These energies and enthusiasms did not easily die, and we have proof in the poetry of Shelley that the French Revolution still seemed, in spite of its failure, to be a great example of a struggle for liberty, and a powerful portent of what man could achieve. Indeed, to Shelley, the French Revolution was more than a passing example; it became the inspiration of his life.

Harriet Shelley was well aware how important the emotions aroused by the French Revolution were to her husband. She knew the appeal that anything connected with revolutionary ideals had for him. When asked by Peacock, the author, what Shelley could see in Mary, Godwin's daughter, Harriet replied, *'Nothing, but that her name was Mary, and not only Mary, but Mary Wollstonecraft.'*

Like Paine, Shelley most earnestly desired constitutional reform and an end to monarchy, which he saw as mere tyranny. In one of his earliest works, 'Queen Mab', written in 1812, he describes a king as:

> *the wearer of a gilded chain*
> *That binds his soul to abjectness, the fool*
> *Whom courtiers nickname monarch, whilst a slave*
> *Even to the basest appetites.*[3]

Similar anti-monarchist ideas were expressed in Keats' early verse, such as the sonnet 'On Peace' in 1814, where he prays:

> *O Europe! Let not sceptred tyrants see*
> *That thou must shelter in thy former state,*

or in a poem written in 1815 on the anniversary of Charles the Second's Restoration which he calls Britain's *'direst, foulest shame'*. But while Keats concentrated more and more on the meaning of poetry itself, and on his search for his own fulfilment as a poet, Shelley's writing continued to be often overtly political.

Often, too, he was directly influenced by the French Revolution. Although usually thought of as a poet, Shelley was a great writer of political pamphlets, and in his *Address to the Irish People* he begged them not to repeat the mistakes of the French:

> *Never do evil that good may come,*

he advised, pointing out that,

> *The French Revolution, although undertaken with the best*
> *intentions, ended ill for the people, because violence was*
> *employed.*

Later the same year, 1812, he issued a *Declaration of Rights*, in the manner of the French Revolutionary Assembly, or of Tom Paine. This began uncompromisingly:

> *Government has no rights; it is a delegation from several*
> *individuals for the purpose of securing their own,*

and went on to declare that

> *Titles are tinsel, power a corruption, glory a bubble, and*
> *excessive wealth a libel on its possessor.*

But while influenced by the reforming zeal of the French Revolution, Shelley was convinced that it had failed because of its use of violence. His *Declaration of Rights* states explicitly, *'Man has no right to kill his brother'*. Soldiers are not exempted; on the contrary, to kill in uniform *'adds the infamy of servitude to the crime of murder'*. Shelley was convinced that the spirit of liberty could prevail by the power of love and harmony within itself.

The poem which exhibits most clearly his vision of a bloodless revolution is 'The Revolt of Islam', written in 1817, to show, Shelley said, that *'Love is . . . the sole law which should govern the moral world'*. The poem tells how Laon, an ardent and heroic young man, and Cythna, an inspiring and fervent young woman, find that they love each other and love the cause of liberty and equality. They separate, to spread the word to the downtrodden masses throughout the world, but, after much suffering, they meet again in the city of a notorious tyrant, where Cythna, now calling herself Laone, is inspiring the slaves to take their freedom. Unlike the French Revolution, in this uprising the insurgents are peaceful, offering brotherly love to all; and unlike the leaders in France, Laon and Cythna are martyred by the tyrant, but find happiness and an ideal existence beyond death—in what is to all intents and purposes heaven, in spite of Shelley's antichristian doctrine.

In the first canto of 'The Revolt of Islam', Shelley quite explicitly outlines his debt to the French Revolution:

> *When first the living blood through all these veins*
> *Kindled a thought in sense, great France sprang forth*
> *And seized, as if to break, the ponderous chains*
> *Which bind in woe the nations of the earth.*
> *I saw, and started from my cottage-hearth;*
> *And to the clouds and waves in tameless gladness*
> *Shrieked, till they caught immeasurable mirth.*[4]

However, Shelley explains that now France's great moment has passed:

> *When the last hope of trampled France had failed*
> *Like a brief dream of unremaining glory,*
> *From visions of despair I rose.*[5]

The French Revolution had seemed a glorious vision, but it had failed: Shelley now hoped to inspire a new, successful, but bloodless, revolution by his poetry.

The two themes which occur in almost all Shelley's work are the misery of present society, with its intolerance (sometimes resulting in the martyrdom of the hero or heroine, representing Shelley) and the beautiful new world which is to come. He felt that some sort of crisis must occur—hopefully a peaceful revolution, but, if not, then a violent one. In his essay 'A Philosophical View of Reform', written in 1819, he states immediately that, with the exception of those whose interests are shielded by the Establishment,

> *there is no inhabitant of the British Empire of mature age and perfect understanding not fully persuaded of the necessity of Reform,*

and he warns—

> *the sure character of misgovernment is misery, and first dis-*

*content and, if that be despised, then insurrection, as the
legitimate expression of that misery.*

His famous sonnet 'England in 1819' sums up his bitter views of his
country's wretchedness:

> *An old, mad, blind, despised and dying king,—*
> *Princes, the dregs of their dull race, who flow*
> *Through public scorn—mud from a muddy spring—*
> *Rulers who neither see, nor feel, nor know,*
> *But leech-like to their fainting country cling,*
> *Till they drop, blind in blood, without a blow,—*
> *A people starved and stabbed in the untilled field,—*
> *An army, which liberticide and prey*
> *Makes as a two-edged sword to all who wield,—*
> *Golden and sanguine laws which tempt and slay;*
> *Religion Christless, Godless—a book sealed;*
> *A Senate,—Time's worst statute unrepealed,—*
> *Are graves, from which a glorious Phantom may*
> *Burst, to illumine our tempestuous day.*

Shelley's disgust with contemporary society led him to formulate
an ideal state where all abuses and vices could be done away with.
A glimpse of this paradise can be seen in *Prometheus Unbound* where
the Spirit of the Hour describes her vision of the new order:

> *And behold, thrones were kingless, and men walked*
> *One with the other even as spirits do,*
> *None fawned, none trampled; hate, disdain, or fear,*
> *Self-love or self-contempt, on human brows*
> *No more inscribed . . .*
> *Thrones, altars, judgement-seats, and prisons; wherein*
> *And besides which, by wretched men were borne*
> *Sceptres, tiaras, swords, and chains and tomes*
> *Of reasoned wrong, glozed on by ignorance . . .*
> *Stand, not o'erthrown, but unregarded now . . .*
> *The loathsome mask has fallen, the man remains*
> *Sceptreless, free, uncircumscribed, but man*
> *Equal, unclassed, tribeless, and nationless,*
> *Exempt from awe, worship, degree, the king*
> *Over himself.*[6]

Optimist that he was, Shelley reckoned without human nature;
his plans for a world different from the world he saw, depended on

men being different from what their human nature caused them to be. He had a deep faith that he, in the guise of a Laon, a Cythna or a Prometheus, could reform the world by the persuasion of his poetry, as Laon, stabbed by a spear, pleads to friends and enemies alike to be reconciled to each other by his words.

Eventually, however, it seems that Shelley had to admit, even to himself, that, like the French Revolution, his dreams were doomed to failure. In 'The Revolt of Islam', the new world is established temporarily on earth, but is seen as permanently established only beyond death. In *Prometheus Unbound* it is only when the millennium eventually arrives that the martyr-hero is released. In both these poems, Shelley sees his new world as an ideal, not actually attainable, in any real sense, on earth. Earlier in his life, in 'Queen Mab', Shelley had foretold that it was *on earth* that the reform should take place:

> *How sweet a scene will Earth become!*
> *Of purest spirits a pure dwelling-place,*
> *Symphonious with the planetary spheres;*
> *When man, with changeless Nature coalescing,*
> *Will undertake regeneration's work.*[7]

But by 1819, when he wrote his Preface to *Prometheus Unbound*, he was to admit that although his hero showed what could be achieved, he himself was not writing didactic poetry, but putting forward *'idealisms'*. He says that he has *'a passion for reforming the world'* but denies that he considers his poetry *'in any degree as containing a reasoned system on the theory of human life'*. He is, he claims, writing *'beautiful idealisms of moral excellence'*.

Disillusioned with English society, disillusioned by the outcome of the French Revolution, disillusioned with mankind in general, Shelley felt that his perfect state was an *'idealism'*, and yet at moments he had thought it to be an idealism that could be achieved and fulfilled. Man might be in slavery now; but *'if winter comes, can spring be far behind?'*

---

[1] T. J. Hogg *The Life of Shelley* in *The Life of Percy Bysshe Shelley* (2 vols) (Dent, 1933) p. 304   [2] William Wordsworth *The Prelude* Book IX, 522–531   [3] 'Queen Mab' III, 30–33   [4] 'The Revolt of Islam' Canto I, XXXIX   [5] *ibid.* Canto I, I   [6] *Prometheus Unbound* Act III, scene IV, 131–5; 164–7; 179; 193–7   [7] 'Queen Mab' VI, 39–43

4

Industrial and Agrarian Revolutions: Social Changes

The period from mid-eighteenth to mid-nineteenth century was, as we saw in the previous chapter, a time of immense political upheaval, when ideas and systems throughout Europe were overturned and re-evaluated. More importantly, perhaps, for Britain, it was a time of great social change, when the day-to-day business of living was completely altered for thousands of workers, and the old order of things was bewilderingly transformed. These social changes occurred largely as a result of the movements known to historians as the Industrial and Agrarian Revolutions, through which British agriculture became highly organized and British industry became the most mechanized and profitable in the world.

Why these changes, particularly the Industrial Revolution, should have occurred in Britain rather than elsewhere, and in Britain at that particular time, is a matter of debate. Many complex factors were involved, but E. J. Hobsbawm points out in *Industry and Empire* that:

> *The main preconditions for industrialization were already present in eighteenth-century Britain, or could be easily brought into being.*

There was sufficient available capital for *'economic transformation'*, and *'transport and communications were comparatively easy and cheap'*. Moreover, Britain already possessed men who had practical experience of simple machinery, and who could turn their talents to mechanizing industry.

On the agricultural side, too, Britain was prepared for greater efficiency and commercial success, for as Hobsbawm remarks, *'Farming was already predominantly for the market'*. The need to feed a growing population—and in wartime, under blockade conditions, to survive on home-produced food—meant that improved techniques were not merely desirable, but essential. Developments such as Jethro Tull's seed-drill, and the new Rotherham plough, together with the use of turnips and clover to remove the need for fallow fields, led to increased crop production, while careful stockbreeding meant more and better meat. Small farmers who had lived a hand-to-mouth existence became suddenly more aware, especially in the period of soaring wartime prices, that their land was a source of profit.

Profit was also the immediate result of industrialization. Fortunes were made in a few years by men with foresight and a little capital, like the industrialist Robert Owen, who saw the possibilities of such inventions as Hargreaves' Spinning Jenny. The production of cotton cloth was revolutionized by mechanization; from being a cottage industry carried on by spinning-wheel and handloom, it gradually became completely factory-based, and Britain's import of raw cotton increased twelve times over between 1760 and 1830, contributing enormously to the country's export trade, and bringing great wealth to the factory owners.

But although greater efficiency and mechanization in town and country increased production, and could be seen as bringing long-term national benefits, in the short-term there was one immediate effect: the desire for profit began to control society. Expediency became all-important, and human considerations were sacrificed to the profit motive.

In agriculture, this was seen most clearly in the spate of enclosures. At the beginning of the eighteenth century, much agricultural land was still farmed as it had been for centuries—that is, it was divided into strips of uneconomic size farmed by peasants on a subsistence basis. Gradually it came to be realized that larger units were needed, especially if new techniques were to be put into practice, and manorial lords applied to Parliament to enclose land, especially common land. But, as corn prices increased, particularly in the boom time of the French wars, grasping farmers enclosed all available land, not with a view to long-term agricultural improvement, but with a view to a quick profit. Suddenly, instead of farming for themselves, albeit on a tiny piece of land, villagers found that they were labourers, subject to seasonal employment—and unemployment. While the landlords gained, the labourer lost the grazing land on which he might have kept an animal or two—and, more importantly, he lost all sense of independence. As E. P. Thompson explains in *The Making of the English Working Class*:

> The arguments of the enclosure propagandists were commonly phrased in terms of higher rental values and higher yield per acre. In village after village, enclosure destroyed the scratch-as-scratch-can economy of the poor.

The precarious hand-to-mouth existence of the small tenant farmer might have seemed undesirable, but it had a sense of purpose. The growing industrial towns bought up food in large quantities from the rural areas, and any surplus which the small tenant farmer might produce could be sold at the local market for his own gain. But when such tenants became labourers in the larger, more economic units created by enclosure, they were acutely aware that the surplus food they produced now became part of the landlord's profit. William Cobbett, whom Hazlitt called *'not only unquestionably the most powerful political writer of the present day, but one of the best writers in the language'*, commenting upon the lot of such agricultural labourers in his *Rural Rides*, remarks that:

> *the poor creatures that raise the wheat and the barley and cheese and the mutton and the beef are living upon potatoes ... all is done* according to law *... but, somehow or other, the produce is, at last,* carried away, *and it is eaten for the main part, by those who do not work.*

Nor was it only enclosure which brought immediate suffering; the industrial revolution impinged upon the countryside when textile processes began to be reproduced by machines in factories instead of by hand in cottages. The *'Lords of the Loom'* as Cobbett called the manufacturers, caused the country people to:

> *lose part of their natural employment. The women and children who ought to provide the great part of the raiment, have nothing to do. The fields* must have men and boys; *but, where there are men and boys there will be* women *and girls; and, as the Lords of the Loom have now a set of* real slaves, *by the means of whom they take away a great part of the unemployment of the* country-women and girls, *these must be kept by poor-rates.*

The Poor Rates were themselves a cause of misery. Each parish was responsible for its own paupers and consequently strongly discouraged the arrival of any poor stranger. This meant that labourers could not easily move to areas where jobs and food might be more abundant. The poet Robert Southey, brother-in-law of Samuel Taylor Coleridge, describes this graphically in his *Letters from England*:

> *as each parish is bound to provide for its own poor, an endless source of oppression and litigation arises from the necessity of*

*keeping out all persons likely to become chargeable. . . . If . . .
they endeavour to remove to some situation where . . . work is
more plentiful, or provisions cheaper, the overseers are alarmed,
the intruder is apprehended as if he were a criminal, and sent
back to his own parish.*[1]

10. *William Cobbett*, artist unknown. William Cobbett began writing as a Tory,
but soon adopted radical views and vigorously urged Parliamentary reform.
(National Portrait Gallery, London)

Coleridge, too, described the misery caused by the bad administration of the Poor Laws, where the farmers, who paid much of the relief money, were more concerned about cash than kindness. He also attacked the Speenhamland System, first applied in 1795 at Speenhamland in Berkshire, whereby poor labourers' wages were supplemented from the Poor Rates. This seemed at first sight a beneficial idea but in practice it encouraged farmers to hold down wages while letting the whole parish contribute to Poor Relief; and labourers were humiliated by having to accept charity instead of the rightful rate for their work. *'Let it not be forgotten'*, wrote Coleridge,

> *that in agricultural districts three fourths of the Poors' Rates are paid to healthy, robust and (O sorrow and shame!) industrious hard-working Paupers in lieu of wages.*[2]

Cobbett also attacked the same iniquity:

> *The labourer must have his belly full and be free from fear and this bellyfull must come to him from out of his wages, and not from benevolence of any description.*

As enclosures and agricultural mechanization proceeded, then, the farmers gained and the labourers grew more desperate. Their miseries seemed to grow in proportion as their masters benefited; enclosure led to greater profit for the landlords, while the difficulties of the workers were increased by such restrictions as the savage game laws which made poaching on the enclosed lands an extremely hazardous undertaking. That many were driven to risk the penalties is obvious from Cobbett's comment that *'the game-laws . . . put into the gaols* a full third part of the prisoners'.

Another burden on the poor, and one which Cobbett particularly objected to, was the duty of paying tithes to the clergyman holding the living of a parish, whether he actually resided there or not. This was seen as a further example of the exploitation of the poor by the rich, since clergymen were part of the establishment and livings were often held for the younger sons of noble families—as, for example, Jane Austen depicts in *Mansfield Park* where the livings of Mansfield and Thornton Lacey are both in the gift of Sir Thomas and are held for Edmund Bertram; or in *Pride and Prejudice* where Mr Collins, talking of the many duties of a rector, notes that:

> *In the first place, he must make such an agreement for tythes as may be beneficial to himself and not offensive to his patron.*

Cobbett had no doubts about the iniquity both of tithes and of patronage, which he saw as simple exploitation of the poor labourers by very rich parasites:

> *It is a part of our system to have certain* families *who have no particular merit; but who are to be maintained, without why or wherefore, at the public expense. . . . They seem to be a sort of creatures that have an* inheritance in the public carcass, *like the magots that some people have in their skin.*

Standing on a hill above Dover, he reflects on the difference at harvest-time between England, with its exploited poor, and post-Revolutionary France:

> *I saw the parsons's shocks of wheat and barley, left in the field after the farmer had taken his away. Turning my head, and looking across the Channel, 'There,' said I, pointing to France, 'there the spirited and sensible people have ridded themselves of this burden . . . the French farmer . . . has* no tithes to pay.*

Tithes, game laws, rising prices, low wages, unemployment, loss of cottage industry, enclosure—the hardships of the farm labourer at this time seem vicious, even if, unlike Cobbett, we are prepared to admit long-term benefits of the Agrarian Revolution. But historians are in doubt about one effect—to what extent did these conditions drive labourers from the land to the towns? It is certain that the towns expanded enormously at this time. At the beginning of the eighteenth century, London, with a population of 600,000, had been twenty times as large as Bristol, the second biggest city; but a hundred years later, Sheffield was almost as big as Bristol had been in 1801, and Birmingham, Manchester and Liverpool were well over twice as big as Sheffield. However, this was not necessarily due only to a huge influx of labourers from the land, for there was in any case a rapidly rising population.

But for the farm worker who did leave the land and move to one of the industrial centres, life was not easy and old problems were replaced by new ones. By the first decade of the nineteenth century, new techniques in the textile industry meant the concentration of spinning and weaving in factories, near coalfields supplying power for the steam engines that worked the mills. In the iron industry too, innovations meant the removal of workshops from isolated woodland areas to cluster round the mines. Charcoal had been the basis of the smelting process, but after 1783 when Cort had perfected his technique for melting and stirring iron—the 'puddling and rolling' process—using coke furnaces, coal became the main fuel of the iron industry; and so the coal industry, too, began to expand. From this time the growth of the northern towns, in previously sparsely populated areas, was inevitable, and conurbations sprang up which offered the minimum living conditions to the maximum number of workers:

> The dwellings of the labouring manufacturers [i.e. the workers],

wrote Robert Southey in his Letters from England,

> are in narrow streets and lanes, blocked up from light and air
> ... crowded together because every inch of land is of such value,
> that room for light and air cannot be afforded them.[3]

It must be admitted that such conditions were by no means deliberate. Indeed, in the early days of industrialization when factory owners wished to attract employees to their mills, the brick-built accommodation they offered as a temptation to country people, often still used to wattle-and-daub houses, seemed palatial indeed. Arkwright's town of Cromford, for example, still contains some of the strong, well-built houses offered to his mill workers. But as the second and third generation of workers arrived, and as the move from country to town increased, the accommodation provided simply could not cope with the numbers who occupied it. Worse, the problems of water supply and sewage disposal, relatively easily dealt with in small villages, became a matter for large-scale organization in the rapidly growing towns, but the large-scale organization simply was not there to deal with it. Local corporations did not exist to provide the kind of facilities which we associate with urban living today. Consequently, by inevitable accident rather than design, the conditions which farm labourers met on arrival in the towns were appalling; but then there was the attraction of a regular wage to tempt them.

However, the conditions in which the workers were employed were also deplorable, and while spinners worked long hours in temperatures of 27°C, they could be fined for opening a window, taking time off for a quick wash—or even whistling to relieve the monotony. Women and children were exploited by being given low wages for their excruciating labour. Children worked twelve or thirteen hours a day, from the age of five or six, and as conditions worsened in the countryside, parishes happily sent poor children to be 'apprentices' in the factories, to relieve the parish of the burden. In 1802, in an attempt to improve the lot of these apprentices, an Act was passed restricting their working day to only twelve hours between the times of 6 a.m. and 9 p.m. But this was thought too liberal for many factory owners, who thereupon ceased taking apprentices and employed 'free labour'—that is, children who were free to leave at any time (though if they did, there would be no employment for them elsewhere), and therefore received no protection in law.

As water power was replaced by steam power, so that the factories congregated near the mining-towns, women and children were increasingly employed down the mines, pulling the coal-wagons. This was gruelling work—and hazardous, too. Davy's safety-lamp, invented in 1815, at first eased the dangers somewhat, but later encouraged profit-seeking mine owners to sink deeper shafts in more dangerous areas. Considerations of safety, of humanity, and of duty to one's workers, were often abandoned in industry, as they were in agriculture, if they conflicted with the chance of financial gain.

Britain grew in material wealth, but, as an increasing number of thinking men—industrialists as well as poets, conservatives as well as radicals—began to see, she was losing immeasurably in a spiritual sense. What Thomas Carlyle later called 'the cash nexus' was becoming the only link between master and man. Human ties were debased, as the relationship between employer and employee became strictly a matter of cash. 'I see clearly', wrote the poet Wordsworth in 1817, at a time when his early democratic fervour had long since abated but his love of humanity had not,

> that the principal ties which kept the different classes of society in a vital and harmonious dependence upon each other have, within these thirty years, either been greatly impaired or wholly dissolved. Everything has been put up to market and sold for the highest price it would buy. Farmers used formerly to be attached to their landlords, and labourers to their farmers who employed them. All that kind of feeling has vanished—in like manner, the connexion between the trading and the landed interests of country towns undergoes no modification from personal feeling. . . . All . . . moral cement is dissolved, habits and prejudices are broken and rooted up, nothing being substituted in their place but a quickened self-interest.[4]

The danger, as the philanthropic industrialist Robert Owen saw it, was that avid attention was given to the smooth running of the 'dead machinery' while the 'living machinery' was neglected and disregarded. For most factory workers, their way of life had undergone an unprecedented and traumatic change; instead of feeling a certain dignity and independence, though subject to the changes of weather and the seasons, they were now subject to factory managers and overseers who expected them to arrive at set times, and work set hours. Even the natural system of daylight working was overcome by the new gas-lighting in factories. Furthermore, while the farm labourer might have a small piece of land to cultivate in order to supplement his income, the factory-worker had nothing except his labour to offer, and he was consequently forced to sell himself to the highest bidder—like a slave, as many contemporary writers remarked, often adding, like Owen, that the slaves in the West Indies were:

> *much better provided for than . . . these oppressed and degraded children and workpeople in the home manufacturies of Great Britain.*

Some enlightened industrialists sincerely tried to overcome the wretchedness of factory life. Robert Owen astounded his competitors by proving at the New Lanark Mills that with benevolent methods his workers not only equalled the output and quality of other factories, but did much better. Child labour was stopped in the New Lanark plant, and free full-time education was provided up to the age of ten. But Owen alienated the other manufacturers by proposing co-operative schemes where there would be no personal profit—an unthinkable suggestion to most 'Lords of the Loom', who must have been considerably relieved when Owen's attempts to found experimental communes failed. As it was, in many factories the 'living machines' continued to be treated rather worse than the 'dead' ones.

The love of humanity expressed by poets such as Blake, Wordsworth, Coleridge, Southey, and later Keats and Shelley, is directed vehemently against this dehumanizing effect of commerce. Blake, Keats and Shelley may be termed radicals; Wordsworth, Coleridge and Southey became right-wing after some youthful dallyings at the other extreme. But their message is unanimous and insistent; the profit-motive destroys all worthwhile human feeling:

> *Where any view of Money exists, Art cannot be carried on,*[5]

wrote Blake, to be echoed by Wordsworth's sonnet which begins:

> *The world is too much with us; late and soon*
> *Getting and spending, we lay waste our powers,*

and by Shelley's outcry against:

> *Commerce! beneath whose poison-breathing shade*
> *No solitary virtue dares to spring,*
> *But Poverty and Wealth with equal hand*
> *Scatter their withering curses.*[6]

To Blake, to Shelley (much influenced by Godwin—and perhaps by his own frequent financial embarrassments) and to Keats, who declared he had no idea of controlling finances, money was a real source of evil. As life in the newly industrialized society became more materialistic, as personal relationships were subject to the harsh impersonal reality of factory life, so cash seemed to matter more and more, and people less and less. The Romantic visionaries, both Tory and Jacobin, saw village life—where a certain amount of barter and a large amount of payment in kind had reduced the need for money to intrude too much— being replaced by the new agricultural system of a farmer paying cash wages supplemented by cash Poor Relief; or else saw cottagers, who had worked in their own homes and at their own pace at spinning wheels and looms, driven into factories where harsh conditions of work were rigidly enforced in return for standard payments—often to be traded only in the factory tommy-shops.

They saw, too, that all dignity of labour had gone, and work was merely a pointless but financially necessary task. Blake saw the monotony of factory existence as a nightmare world of futility:

> *intricate wheels invented, wheel without wheel,*
> *To perplex youth in their outgoings and to bind to labours in*
>   *Albion*
> *Of day and night the myriads of eternity: that they may grind*
> *And polish brass and iron hour after hour, laborious task,*
> *Kept ignorant of its use: that they might spend the days of*
>   *wisdom*
> *In sorrowful drudgery to obtain a scanty pittance of bread,*
> *In ignorance to view a small portion and think that All.*[7]

The qualities which made men human were, they felt, being totally eradicated. As man grasped for more and more money, he lost his hold on all that was of real importance. Man regarded fellow man, not as his brother, but as a potential source of exploited wealth, to be ruthlessly suppressed and oppressed. So Blake saw it, in 'The Song of Los':

Shall not the Councellor throw his curb
Of Poverty on the laborious?
To fix the price of labour,
To invent allegoric riches,

And the privy admonishers of men
Call for fires in the City,
For heaps of smoking ruins
In the night of prosperity and wantonness

To turn man from his path,
To restrain the child from the womb,
To cut off the bread from the city
That the remnant may learn to obey.

And yet, as Robert Owen saw, commerce itself need not bring misery. Rightly used, it could set up a new society, of the sort that Southey and Coleridge had dreamed of founding on the banks of the Susquehanna, or which Shelley imagined in 'Queen Mab'. According to Owen's autobiography Britain's industry had brought her great wealth, providing:

> the most ample means to educate, employ, place and govern, the whole population of the British Empire, so as to make all into full-formed, highly intelligent, united and permanently prosperous and happy men and women.

Southey also saw that although there was extreme poverty here— *'nor is poverty anywhere else attended with such actual suffering'*— Britain was a very rich country, whose wealth was *'the envy of the rest of Europe'*.

If industrialization could produce such wealth, then why was there such poverty? Contemporary observers are unanimous in pointing out the simple but deplorable fact that profits from the labour of many were directed into the pockets of the few. *'There is no real wealth but the labour of man'*, wrote Shelley in 1813 in his Notes on 'Queen Mab', adding bitterly that:

> wealth is a power usurped by the few to compel the many to labour for their benefit.

Southey felt that the manufacturers, the *'Lords of the Loom'* were to blame, and that they deliberately kept their workers *'miserably poor'* in order to ensure obedience:

> *They would not be crowded in hot task-houses by day, and
> herded together in unwholesome employment from sunrise till
> sunset . . . before furnaces which are never suffered to cool . . .
> the poor would never do these things unless they were miserably
> poor, unless they were in that state of abject poverty which
> precludes instruction, and by destroying all hope for the future,
> reduces men, like the brutes, to seek for nothing beyond the
> gratification of present wants.*[8]

But the factory owners were not the sole, or even the main, cause
of the trouble. The wages they could pay, and the constancy of
employment, depended upon consistent trade. At times, there was
great demand for goods, and many more workers were employed.
But then later, as for example in the slump following the French
wars, unemployment was rife. As Hobsbawm points out in *The Age of
Revolution*, the 1815 Corn Laws, brought in by a Parliament of
landlords to protect landlords from price fluctuation, threatened
British exports and hence British workers:

> *For if the rest of the not yet industrialized world was prevented
> from selling its agrarian products, how was it to pay for the
> manufactured goods which Britain alone could—and had to
> —supply? Manchester business therefore became the centre of
> militant and increasingly desperate opposition to landlordism
> in general and the Corn Laws in particular.*

That the landlords were protected from recession was hard
enough; this was made doubly bitter by the fact that no redress was
open to the exploited poor, since the landlords controlled the seats
in Parliament, and had forbidden a united labouring voice by passing Combination Acts in 1799 and 1800 to ban trade unions. Furthermore, landlords seemed to be protected, at least partially, at all
times; during the French wars, when corn prices rose, the landowners made vast fortunes, while for the poor this meant increased
bread prices. When the post-war slump came, they passed the
Corn Laws. This situation was bitterly reviewed by Thomas
Bewick, a wood-engraver who was acquainted with Keats and
Haydon and who wrote his *Memoirs* in the period just after the
Napoleonic Wars. During the French wars, he writes:

> *Estates rose in value to an extraordinary height, and the price
> of grain etc., still more so. The shipping interest wallowed in
> riches; the gentry whirled about in aristocratic pomposity;
> they forgot what their demeanour and good, kind behaviour*

used to be to those in inferior stations in life, and seemed now
far too often to look upon them like dirt. . . . When peace came,
it brought with it a sudden fall in the price of corn . . . they
mostly deserved this reverse of fortune. Not so with the
industrious labourer. His privations were great, and he was
undeservedly doomed to suffer for want of employment and
often to waste away and die of hunger and want.

11. *The House of Commons* by K. A. Hickel, 1793. Parliament at the end of the
eighteenth century consisted largely of landowners, who were often suspected of
acting in their own interests rather than considering the well-being of the majority
of their countrymen. (National Portrait Gallery, London)

Giotian was here

Cobbett, too, in his *Rural Rides*, often comments bitterly on the
abundance and fertility of the vales through which he passes, compared with the privations and dejection of the agricultural workers
who so obviously do not partake of the profits which their exploited
labour creates. '*This is,*' he remarked angrily, '*I verily believe it, the*
worst used labouring people upon the face of the earth.'

Exploitation was Shelley's constant theme too. If real wealth lay
in labour, the labourers should reap the benefits, as he stated firmly
in 'Song to the Men of England', written in 1819:

Men of England, wherefore plough
For the lords who lay ye low?

*Wherefore weave with toil and care
The rich robe your tyrants wear? . . .*

*The seed ye sow another reaps;
The wealth ye find, another keeps;
The robes ye weave, another wears;
The arms ye forge, another bears.*

*Sow seed—but let no tyrant reap;
Find wealth—let no imposter heap;
Weave robes—let not the idle wear;
Forge arms—in your defence to bear.*

The rising prices by which manufacturers, supplying arms and
munitions, and landlords, controlling food production, benefited
during the French wars, were seen by many as exploitation of a
peculiarly vile kind; for until the rise of Napoleon caused second
thoughts, many writers, particularly of the Romantic school, saw
the new French society as a triumph for the exploited people over
the tyrannous aristocracy, and Britain's entry into the war as a move
by a frightened landed interest to protect itself at all costs. The vast
expenditure of men and money on this war, financed by increased
taxation, was therefore seen as an iniquitous waste authorized by a
government representing minority interests, and as a result of which
only those minority interests could benefit, both financially and
politically. As Owen points out, the need for war materials:

> *created a demand for and gave great encouragement to new
> mechanical inventions and chemical discoveries, to supersede
> manual labour,*

and while mechanization took over the jobs of the labouring poor,
the landed interest could only benefit:

> *The war was a great and most extravagant customer to farmers,
> manufacturers, and other producers of wealth.*

Thomas Bewick was in no doubt that Britain's entry into what he
calls *'this superlatively wicked war'* was a device by those in power to
protect their interests, financed by the wealth of exploited masses:

> *In this state of things, with Mr Pitt at their head, and the
> resources of the British Isles in their hands, it was calculated
> upon as a certainty that his weight added to the already power-
> ful confederacy, would soon put a stop to the march of intellect
> and . . . put an extinguisher upon the rights of man.*

If the money and materials wasted upon the war had been rightly used, he felt, the wealth created by the labourers could have been usefully re-invested in industry, instead of being used to restore a despotic French monarchy. Cobbett, too, rails against the money spent on defences, particularly the Martello Towers along the south coast:

> *I think I have counted along here upwards of thirty of these ridiculous things, which, I dare say, cost five, perhaps ten, thousand pounds each. . . . There is, they say, a chain of these things all the way to Hastings! I dare say they cost MILLIONS. But, far indeed are these from being all, or half, or a quarter of the squandering along here. . . . All along the coast there are works of some sort or other; incessant sinks of money.*

He is similarly scathing both about the cost and scar on the landscape of Dover Castle, and the wastefulness of a scheme *'so scandalously disgraceful'* whereby:

> *more brick and stone have been buried in this hill than would go to build a neat new cottage for every labouring man in the counties of Kent and of Sussex!*

Worst of all, he feels, like Bewick, that this deplorable extravagance was not to protect the people, but only the government:

> *What they wanted, was to prevent the landing, not of Frenchmen, but of French principles; that is to say, to prevent the example of the French from being alluring to the people of England.*

The people were paying to support the very system which oppressed them.

The Romantic writers, too, saw the war as another example of the corrupt power of money. The wealthy gained from the war; the poor, who suffered most, were ruined by it. Commerce and war, felt Blake, were therefore inseparable allies, used by government to keep man in chains:

> *In every cry of every Man*
> *In every Infant's cry of fear,*
> *In every voice, in every ban*
> *The mind-forg'd manacles I hear.*

> *How the Chimney-sweeper's cry*
> *Every black'ning Church appalls,*
> *And the hapless Soldier's sigh*
> *Runs in blood down Palace walls.*[9]

Shelley, too, saw the poor oppressed both by commercial and military interests. In his poem of 1811, 'A Tale of Society as it Is from Facts', he tells of an old woman bowed under the weight of poverty:

> *She was a cripple, and incapable*
> *To add one mite to gold-fed luxury:*
> *And therefore did her spirit dimly feel*
> *That poverty, the crime of tainting stain,*
> *Would merge her in its depths, never to rise again.*
> *One only son's love had supported her. . . .*
> *But, when the tyrant's bloodhounds forced the child*
> *For his cursed power unhallowed arms to yield—*
> *Bend to another's will—become a thing*
> *More senseless than the sword of battlefield—*
> *Then did she feel keen sorrow's keenest sting;*
> *And many years had passed ere comfort they would bring.*[10]

When her son finally returns, he has been broken mentally and physically. War has:

> *Utterly poisoned life's unmingled bowl,*
> *And unsubduable evils on him brought.*[11]

Ironically the pair are compelled to live on Poor Relief, grudgingly administered by the State which has ruined them.

As the Romantic writers and artists saw it, then, the new commercial society which had grown up around them was to be attacked on two counts: it bolstered the rich at the expense of the poor who really created the wealth, and, worse still, it deadened the nation's soul. It was the self-appointed task of the nation's poets to save that soul.

Even feeling that there was a chance of redemption placed them in opposition to popular feeling of the day. Godwin and Shelley, believing in the perfectibility of man, flew in the face of widely-held belief, especially those of the new political economists, such as Ricardo, who maintained that while landowners would increase profits by cultivation, labourers' wages would not improve. The clergyman and economist Malthus painted an even more gloomy picture. He maintained in his *Essay on the Principle of Population* that man would reproduce faster than food supplies and that, unless the population was controlled, mass famine would inevitably result. The measures he advocated to prevent this infuriated humanitarians, who saw them as a further attack on the defenceless poor. A labourer should not marry, said Malthus, unless he could support a family; if he did so, he could *'be considered as an enemy to his fellow labourers'*. Poor Relief should be done away with completely, as it encouraged the poor to breed, while:

> the quantity of provisions consumed in workhouses . . . diminishes the stores that would otherwise belong to more industrious and more worthy members.

Also, Malthus saw benefits in wretchedness, in that it provided objects for charity:

> The sorrow and distresses of life . . . awaken social sympathy . . . generate all the Christian virtues, and . . . afford scope for the ample exertion of benevolence.

It was exactly this solution which Blake had rejected when writing:

> Pity would be no more
> If we did not make somebody poor.[12]

Rejecting the view that man was doomed to misery, and feeling also that the older generation of Romantic poets, particularly Wordsworth and Southey, had betrayed their youthful enthusiasms, Shelley took on the self-appointed task of creating a better society. Keats, too, felt that spiritual values must be revitalized, and he was acutely conscious of human grief. When, in 'The Fall of Hyperion', Keats dreams of his arrival in the temple where, if ever, he is to attain the status of a poet, he is told that:

> None can usurp this height . . .
> But those to whom the miseries of the world
> Are misery, and will not let them rest.[13]

He queries why he is therefore alone, when there are *'thousands'* who *'feel the giant agony of the world'*, and is reminded that:

> Those whom thou spak'st of are no visionaries . . .
> They come not here, they have no thought to come—
> And thou art here, for thou art less than they.[14]

He can do no *'benefit'* to the world, for he is simply *'a dreaming thing'*. Keats is no practical philanthropist, then; indeed, he differs greatly from Shelley in that he does not dream of a millennium. On the contrary, in a long letter to George and Georgiana Keats, he explains why he does not believe in *'perfectibility'*. Man, he says, will always be *'destined to hardships and disquietude of some kind or other'*. This world is:

> the vale of soul-making. . . . Do you not see how necessary a World of Pains and troubles is to school an Intelligence and make it a Soul? A Place where the heart must feel and suffer in a thousand diverse ways![15]

Keats' way of *'benefiting'* the world, then, is to concentrate upon what he calls *'the principle of beauty in all things'*. As we shall see in future chapters, one of his methods is to take us back to the medieval world, to remove us from the sordid present to the splendours of the past, and another is to make us feel the beauties of nature so intensely that we become one with the natural world. His poetry has no overt message—indeed, he writes to John Hamilton Reynolds that:

> Man should not dispute or assert but whisper results to his neighbour.[16]

Shelley was of the opposite mind; his poetry constantly *'disputes'* and *'asserts'*. In some poems, he pictures society as he sees it—vile, wretched, commerce-ridden, king-corrupted. In others, he sees a vision of the new world that could be. In many, the two themes are united—as in 'Queen Mab', or 'The Revolt of Islam', or *Prometheus Unbound*, or *Hellas*. For Shelley, like Blake, saw the poet as a prophet. Furthermore, if, as they both felt, religion as practised in the world was corrupt, priests were tyrants, and even god, in the form of Blake's Urizen or Shelley's Jupiter, was a vicious despot, then the truth-seeking and truth-giving poet must be the new god and take over the revitalized world, like Keats' Apollo or Shelley's Prometheus. Shelley summed up the social role of the poet in his *Defence of Poetry*:

> poets . . . are not only the authors of language and of music . . . they are the institutors of laws and the founders of civil society. . . . A poet participates in the eternal, the infinite and the one . . . . The most unfailing herald, companion and follower of the awakening of a great people to work a beneficial change in opinion or institution is poetry.

Looking around, then, at what Disraeli was later to call the 'Two Nations'—the multitude of the poor and the privileged rich—and acutely aware of *the agonies, the strife of human hearts*', Keats and Shelley embarked, in their different ways, on an attempt to effect that *beneficial change*'.

[1] Robert Southey (ed. by J. Simmons) *Letters from England* (Cresset Press, 1951) p. 143   [2] S. T. Coleridge *The Collected Works of Samuel Taylor Coleridge* (vol. 6) (Routledge and Kegan Paul, 1972) pp. 221–2 [3] as 1, p. 210   [4] William Wordsworth (ed. by P. Wayne) *Letters of Wordsworth* (O.U.P., 1954) p. 149   [5] William Blake 'The Laocoön' 31 [6] 'Queen Mab' V, 44–7   [7] William Blake *Jerusalem* Chapter 3, plate 65, 21–7   [8] as 1, pp. 211–2   [9] William Blake *Songs of Experience* ('London')   [10] 'A Tale of Society as it Is from Facts' 8–23   [11] *ibid.* 63–4   [12] William Blake *Songs of Experience* ('The Human Abstract') [13] 'The Fall of Hyperion' 147–9   [14] *ibid.* 161; 165–6   [15] K. L. pp. 280–2   [16] *ibid.* p. 107

5

The Liberty of the Individual

In the two previous chapters we have seen how, in the later decades of the eighteenth century and the early part of the nineteenth, men and women from all walks and classes of life became disillusioned with the restraint, conformity, materialism and lack of liberty which seemed to have become the inevitable pattern of life. Church and State seemed to embody controls that were at best paternalistic, at worst dictatorial; in reaction, the calls for freedom and greater equality grew steadily more vociferous. These demands generally developed into movements for political liberty exemplified in the bloody struggle for 'liberty, equality and fraternity' known as the French Revolution; or later, after the failure of violent revolution, into working-class agitation and the early trade unions. At the same time, however, reaction against authoritarian control could be seen in a new search for individual expression and a new reliance on individual thought.

A prime mover in both areas of liberty—political and private—was Jean Jacques Rousseau. Born in 1712 in Geneva, his unsatisfactory childhood, miserable adolescence, and a conviction in adulthood that all men rejected him, contributed greatly to his rejection of society and his insistence that man in a state of nature was without evil. In 1762 he published his *Social Contract*, opening with the startling and provocative assertion that *'Man is born free and everywhere he is in chains'*. The main theme of this work is that society gathers together by a contract, under which the ruler is to serve the people, not to dominate and subjugate them. He asserts:

> *The ruler represents the father, the people the children; and
> . . . all are free and equal by birth.*

The only real power in the state should be *'the general will'*, under the *'supreme direction'* of which everyone *'puts in common his person and his powers'*. Unfortunately, in society as it is, the social contract is ignored:

> *Kings want to be absolute; and from afar men cry out to them*

*that the best way to do this is to make themselves beloved of
their people. This precept is admirable, and in some respects
it is even very true. Unfortunately it will always be the
laughing-stock of courts. . . . Their personal interest is primar-
ily that the people should be weak and wretched, and ever
incapable of resisting them.*

Rousseau goes on to make a point which was to be equally strongly held by Shelley. This was that to be a monarch was, paradoxically,
to be a slave—a slave to custom, courts, ambition, and one's own
passions. *'One thinks himself master of others'*, wrote Rousseau, *'but
is himself the greater slave'*, adding pungently:

> *In the case of a man brought up to rule others, almost every-
> thing conspires to deprive him of justice and reason.*

Another of Rousseau's ideas which was fervently held by Shelley
was that as Christianity taught men to *'turn the other cheek'* and to
value meekness, it was a powerful weapon in the hands of the
Establishment for keeping the masses in subjection. Rousseau saw
this as a matter of plain commonsense:

> *Christianity preaches only servitude and dependence. Its
> spirit is too favourable to tyranny for tyranny not to profit
> always by it.*

These ideas, so strongly asserting the equality of all men and so
strongly denying the power and privileges of Church and King,
were to have an enormous effect on the future of France, confirming
as they did the already fermenting revolutionary feelings which were
to erupt in 1789. More immediately, however, they caught and
underlined a mood of growing unrest several thousand miles away—
in the British colonies on the east coast of America.

The growing numbers of settlers in these 'thirteen colonies' had,
by the very nature of their existence, to foster a spirit of independence and self-reliance. And yet over several decades they were
reminded only too forcibly of the control exercised over their lives
by the British King and Parliament. Under the Stuart monarchs,
legislation had been enacted which gave Britain the monopoly of
trade with her colonies; and the colonies undoubtedly were a useful
market for British manufactured goods. However, in spite of such
close economic liaison, the colonists were not represented in
Parliament at Westminster, and it was this grievance which they
chose as their main objection to paying the duty imposed by the

Stamp Act of 1765. The cry went up from the colonists of 'No taxation without representation'.

The colonists were more incensed when, after the Stamp Act had been withdrawn, an Act of 1767 imposed a tax on some goods imported into the colonies. This Act was in turn repealed in 1770 —except the tax on tea, which was the cause of the famous 'Boston Tea Party' in 1773. Although tea was allowed in more cheaply, as the one item to be taxed its import provided revenue for the government. Significantly, the local men dressed as Red Indians who tipped the tea into Boston Harbour were members of a group styling themselves 'The Sons of Liberty'.

To the British Government, who had recently heard the cry of 'Wilkes and Liberty' (see Chapter 3) in the streets of London only too frequently, the idea of colonial freedom was unthinkable, and they retaliated by a series of Acts designed to quell the rebels of Boston and Massachusetts. But the colonists were by now less interested in their right of representation in the British Parliament than in their natural rights of liberty and equality, as Rousseau had depicted them. Meeting in Philadelphia in 1774, representatives of the colonists issued a Declaration of Rights, and if further evidence was needed that the American states wanted their liberty, it came in 1775 at Lexington, when hostilities broke out between the 'rebels' and the troops of the British Governor. The War of Independence which followed lasted until 1783.

While many Englishmen felt that the colonists were simply rebels, and that they should be made to contribute financially to Britain who bore the cost of defending them, many others had great sympathy with the Americans. Edmund Burke, who, as we saw in Chapter 3, later opposed the violence of the French Revolution, clearly saw the validity of the colonists' claim for 'no taxation without representation'. He appealed for justice and liberty, and in March, 1775, reminded Parliament that they should:

> *Let the colonies always keep the idea of their civil rights associated with your government. . . . As long as you have the wisdom to keep the sovereign authority of this country as the sanctuary of liberty, the sacred temple consecrated to our common faith, wherever the chosen race and sons of England worship freedom, they will turn their faces towards you . . . the more ardently they love liberty, the more perfect will be their obedience. Slavery they can have anywhere. . . . But until you become lost to all feeling of your true interest and your natural dignity, freedom they can have from none but you.*[1]

The Scottish economist, Adam Smith, in his influential work *The Wealth of Nations*, published in 1776, warned that the growing feelings of individualism and independence in the colonists should not be underrated:

> *They are very weak who flatter themselves that, in the state to which things have come, our colonies will be easily conquered by force alone. The persons who now govern the resolutions of what they call their continental congress, feel in themselves at this moment a degree of importance which, perhaps, the greatest subjects in Europe scarcely feel. From shopkeepers, tradesmen and attornies, they are become statesmen and legislators, and are employed in contriving a new form of government for an extensive empire, which . . . seems very likely to become one of the greatest and most formidable that ever was in the world.*

In Britain, then, America was seen, not only as a rebel, but as the cradle of a new sense of individualism and liberty. The American struggle promised hope to all the oppressed. The poet, William Blake, depicted George Washington spurring his people to freedom against the *'heavy iron chain'* which:

> *Descends link by link from Albion's cliffs across the sea to bind Brothers and sons of America, till our faces pale and yellow, Heads deprest, voices meek, eyes downcast, hands work-*
> *bruis'd . . .*
> *Descend to generations that in future times forget.*[2]

But the spirit of America promises liberty, and a new morning of freedom at which all oppressed people may rejoice:

> *Let the slave grinding at the mill run out into the field,*
> *Let him look up into the heavens and laugh in the bright air:*
> *Let the inchained soul, shut up in darkness and in sighing . . .*
> *Rise and look out.*[3]

In America itself, two documents had been produced which were to be of vital significance in the struggle for freedom, both in America and elsewhere. First, in 1776, Tom Paine, who was in America throughout the War of Independence, published *Common Sense*. This pamphlet outlined the weighty reasons which the colonists had for revolt, and urged resistance. America need have no hesitation in declaring her independence, wrote Paine, for Britain had no real interest in her colonies beyond her own financial gain. Having put his case for the colonies, Paine then made an ardent appeal for universal liberty:

> *O ye that love mankind! Ye that dare oppose, not only the tyranny, but the tyrant, stand forth. Every spot of the world is overrun with oppression. Freedom hath been hunted round the globe.*

12. *Thomas Paine* by A. Millière (after an engraving by Romney). Tom Paine, after a vigorous campaign on behalf of the American colonists, took up the battle for liberty again with the publication of his *Rights of Man* in 1791. (National Portrait Gallery, London)

The other important document of 1776 was the Declaration of Independence, drawn up by a Committee and accepted by the Congress of the American colonies on 4 July. The famous lines which declare it to be *'self-evident'* that *'all men are created equal'* are now so well-known that it is easy to forget how very far from self-evident such an assertion would have seemed to many Britons at the time. Equally, the following sentences, which draw a picture of society very like that depicted in Rousseau's *Social Contract*, would then have been highly controversial:

> *all men . . . are endowed by their Creator with certain unalienable rights . . . among these are life, liberty and the pursuit of happiness . . . to secure these rights Governments are instituted among men, deriving their just powers from the consent of the governed . . . whenever any form of government becomes destructive of these ends it is the right of the people to alter or to abolish it, and to institute new government.*

That America thus became synonymous with freedom and liberty can be seen from Shelley's poem of 1817, 'The Revolt of Islam'. As we have seen in Chapter 3, this poem clearly shows the influence upon Shelley of the failure of the French Revolution, but when Laon is pleading for Cythna's life, it is the more successful American struggle for liberty that inspires him:

> *There is a People mighty in its youth,*
> *A land beyond the Oceans of the West,*
> *Where, though with rudest rites, Freedom and Truth*
> *Are worshipped. . . .*
> *That land is like an Eagle, whose young gaze*
> *Feeds on the noontide beam, whose golden plume*
> *Floats moveless on the storm, and in the blaze*
> *Of sunrise gleams when Earth is wrapped in gloom;*
> *An epitaph of glory for the tomb*
> *Of murdered Europe may thy fame be made,*
> *Great People! as the sands shalt thou become;*
> *Thy growth is swift as morn, when night must fade;*
> *The multitudinous Earth shall sleep beneath thy shade. . . .*
> *Nay, start not at the name—America!*[4]

America, then, was seen as the defender of freedom. It had asserted as much in its Declaration of Independence. In 1790, the French sent the key of the Bastille to George Washington to symbolize the American struggle for liberty. But to many American

ᴢᴸ

ᴄ ringing tones of the Declaration of Independence began
now could they assert on the one hand that all men were
free and had the right to liberty, when on the other, these same
ᴄolonists held many thousands of African slaves?

For decades, the slave-trade had flourished between the west
coast of Africa, and the east coast of America and the West Indies.
Millions of slaves were transported the thousands of miles by sea
in the most abominable of conditions, lying flat, chained in layers
on an arrangement of 'shelves' between the decks, subject to all the
privations of filth, malnutrition and disease, and rarely allowed up
on deck because of the tendency of such desperate men and women
to jump overboard rather than suffer the horrors of the 'middle
passage'. By the late eighteenth century it was reckoned that many
tens of thousands of slaves were transported each year, and about
40,000 of them in British ships. Of course, the death rate on board
ship was staggeringly high; also, slaves who seemed in too poor a
condition to fetch much on the market were thrown overboard alive,
this being the quickest way to dispose of them. Once on the American plantations, the negroes were treated as dispensable commodities,
and many planters felt it was better to get a year or two of really hard
work out of a slave, and then replace him, than to encourage a long
working life by better treatment.

At the very time when the American colonists were issuing their
Declaration of Independence, public opinion in Britain was beginning to be roused to the horrors of the trade. Opposition to any
movement to stop the slave-trade, however, came not only from
the distant planters but from the powerful merchants, notably in
Bristol and Liverpool, for whom it represented an extremely profitable business. Nevertheless, men such as James Ramsay, once a
clergyman among planters in the West Indies; John Newton, once
a slave-ship captain himself, now converted and a clergyman;
Granville Sharp, founder-member of the Society for the Abolition
of Slavery; and William Wilberforce, a Member of Parliament and
friend of Pitt; all pledged themselves to the abolition of the trade.
Actually freeing the slaves was seen as a much longer and harder
project; but in the short-term, they could, and would, try to make
the carrying of slaves in British ships illegal.

Various test cases were brought which served both to rouse the
consciences of the British public and to further the cause of the
slaves. The 'Somerset' case in 1772, for example, in which Chief
Justice Mansfield gave the decision that slavery was illegal on
English soil, established an important principle. But just when it

seemed that a move to stop the trade might succeed, the French Revolution broke out, provoking terrified reaction among the British Establishment. Too much liberty was seen as highly dangerous and when William Wilberforce, in April, 1791, asked for permission in Parliament to bring in a Bill which would prohibit the importation of any more slaves into British colonies (though *not* the end of slavery itself) he was heavily defeated, and it was not until 1807 that his idea became law.

13. *The Declaration of Independence* by John Trumbull. This picture by a contemporary American artist captures the sense of purpose and dignity with which the colonists signed their Declaration of Independence from Britain. (Yale University Art Gallery)

Keats and Shelley grew up, therefore, in the period of transition, when the fight to stop the British slave trade was being fought and won, but when British colonists still owned thousands of slaves. Nearer home, as we saw in the previous chapter, they saw the slavery of man to the machine, and felt the chains of custom and materialism fettering society. It is small wonder, then, that the word 'slave' is one of the most frequent in Shelley's poems (though he never takes up the specific case of negro slavery).

Two of the strongest champions of freedom for the negro slaves were clergymen—Ramsay and Newton. Yet to many thinking men at the time the Church itself seemed to exercise a kind of slavery, obsessively demanding conformity, outward at least, to a set of sterile beliefs. In an age when interest in the spiritual and the super-

was growing, the Church, ironically, seemed to have little ᠊ance, and to be too often a tool of the Establishment.

Methodism, the evangelical movement begun by John and Charles Wesley in 1734, was not originally outside the Establishment and did not break away from the Church of England until 1795. Nor was it essentially democratic in its organization. But it did give a new sense of individualism to worship, stressing the equality of all before God. While the search for redemption undoubtedly quelled the dissatisfaction with society in some adherents to Methodism, in others the stress on the equal value of all souls aroused further desire for political equality, while the sense of enthusiasm aroused by the travelling preachers, and the appeal they made to personal emotion, emphasized the growing awareness of the importance of individual feelings.

More revolutionary, however, than a new revival of enthusiasm for Christianity, was the growing movement to deny the claims of established religion altogether. Rousseau had attacked it as a tool of oppression; Paine insisted on *'universal right of conscience'*, stressing that each man should be free to worship God in his own way; and the French Revolutionaries had taken steps to stop all supposedly 'superstitious' practices, including closing the churches. Both Keats and Shelley joined in this attack on the Established Church, though both revered Jesus Himself. Keats wrote of Christ:

> *It is to be lamented that the history of the latter was written and revised by Men interested in the pious frauds of Religion,*[5]

while Shelley described Him as a *'youth with patient looks nailed to a crucifix'*, whose name had *'become a curse'*, for *'the wise, the mild, the lofty and the just'* are persecuted by Christ's *'slaves'* (the priests) for being *'like to'* Him in character.

Reaction against the restraint imposed upon the individual mind by such establishments as the Church revealed itself in a number of ways, all tending more or less to exalt the unconventional, the unexpected, the illogical and the irrational at the expense of the eighteenth-century virtues of reason and order. As we shall see in the next chapter, a new interest in dreams and visions was one manifestation of this reaction; the taste for medievalism, Gothic ruins and horror stories was another, as we shall see in Chapter 7. Further evidence of this delight in the ideas of the individual as opposed to established custom can be seen in the new interest in children, whose minds had before been regarded as undeveloped and untrained, but who from this time on are seen as having a

spontaneity and freshness which are highly desirable. *'The chi
father of the man'*, wrote Wordsworth (inculcating a view that wa
find full expression half a century later in such writers as Dicke
and Charlotte Brontë). And at this time, too, develops the traditi.
of the artist as an outcast from respectable society, living in squalor,
his talents unrecognized but his intellectual integrity superbly
untarnished.

But in Shelley, and to some extent in Keats, we see this reaction
against custom, convention and tyranny in the repeated image of
the one against the many, the weak but determined individual
against powerful opposing forces. For Shelley, of course, it was
more than an idea; he felt himself to be living the part; had he not
been bullied at school, expelled from University, mistreated by his
father, robbed of a parent's rights by the Lord Chancellor and
hounded from his native shores by an unforgiving society? Had he
not stood alone against all the odds? It was only natural that he
should dedicate his poetic talents to the struggle for individual
liberty.

As we have said, the word *'slave'* is one of the most common in
Shelley's poetry. Another is *'tyrant'*. To enumerate the poems in
which these words appear would be to list the majority of Shelley's
works. 'Queen Mab', 'The Revolt of Islam', *Prometheus Unbound*,
The Cenci, Hellas—as well as very many of his short poems—deal
with the theme of the spirit of liberty struggling against oppression.
Almost invariably for Shelley, tyranny is inextricably linked with
custom, with, in fact, the established order of things. It is not the
sudden invasion of a tyrant's army, or the overnight *coup d'état* of
a dictator against which the fight for liberty is joined in Shelley's
poems. On the contrary, it is always a long-established system which
has to be attacked—as, incidentally, it is for Keats in 'Hyperion'—
as habit and tradition (or *'faith'*, as Shelley sometimes called blind
subservience to custom) are the foundation stones of its tyranny.

In 'Queen Mab', for example, Shelley uses the paradox that we
have already noted in Rousseau to show the wretchedness of monarchy. The king is in fact a slave, for he cannot escape the bonds of
custom. He is fettered by tradition as firmly as the meanest slave
is fettered by irons:

> *Is it strange*
> *That, placed on a conspicuous throne of thorns,*
> *Grasping an iron sceptre, and immured*
> *Within a splendid prison, whose stern bounds*

> *Shut him from all that's good or dear on earth,*
> *His soul asserts not its humanity? . . .*
>   *No—'tis not strange.*
> *He like the vulgar, thinks, feels, acts and lives*
> *Just as his father did; the unconquered powers*
> *Of precedent and custom interpose*
> *Between a* King *and virtue.*[6]

In 'The Revolt of Islam', too, the poet describes how tyranny has
been so long established that men no longer think of opposing it:

>   *to abide*
> *That blasting curse men had no shame,*[7]

and men had *'grown hoary In shame and scorn'*. In *The Cenci*, we
learn that the Count has not suddenly become vicious; his youth
was *'dark and fiery'*, *'bold and bad'*, his manhood was *'desperate and
remorseless'*; and now in *'dishonoured age'* he is as dissolute as ever.
Indeed, his only regret is that *'now Invention palls'*, and he would
despair were it not for the fact that he can still think of one

>   *deed to act*
> *Whose horror might make sharp an appetite*
> *Duller than mine.*[8]

In *Hellas* we meet Mahmoud firmly entrenched in power, in a
long-established empire; and in *Prometheus Unbound*, Jupiter the
'almighty tyrant' has ruled for untold ages.

But if time and custom are the friends of tyranny, Shelley also
sees time as ultimately on the side of liberty. Laon and Cythna may
fail, and the Greeks may suffer under Mahmoud; but ultimately all
empires are overthrown. It is a theme he explores at some length in
'Queen Mab', where the Fairy points to ruined civilizations and
shows how man's empires, if corrupt, are doomed to extinction:

> *Once it was the busiest haunt,*
> *Whither, as to a common centre, flocked*
> *Strangers, and ships, and merchandise:*
>   *Once peace and freedom blessed*
>   *The cultivated plain:*
>   *But wealth, that curse of man,*
> *Blighted the bud of its prosperity:*
> *Virtue and wisdom, truth and liberty,*
> *Fled, to return not, until man shall know*

That they alone can give the bliss
  Worthy a soul that claims
  Its kindred with eternity.[9]

The idea of the power of time is, of course, by no means unique
to Shelley. It is a theme beloved of poets and forms the basis of
many Shakespearian sonnets. But it is one which was more important to Shelley, perhaps, than to other writers, for he was not merely
philosophizing on the transience of man; he was waiting for a new
world to come. So, in *Hellas*, at the very point where the Greeks
seem most defeated, and the cry goes up, *'Kill! crush! despoil! Let
not a Greek escape!'*, the Chorus gives the glorious vision of *'A
brighter Hellas'*, *'A loftier Argo'*, and sings with confidence that:

Another Athens shall arise,
And to remoter time
Bequeath, like sunset to the skies,
The splendour of its prime;
And leave, if ought so bright may live,
All earth can take or Heaven can give.[10]

While Keats' poetry was mostly non-political, and his search was
for a higher reality within the imagination, the same discussion, of
time overcoming custom, is sensitively handled in his poem 'Hyperion'. Significantly and symbolically, it is Oceanus, god of the sea
which ebbs and flows, gives and takes away, who points out to the
Titans that all empires must pass away to be replaced by a new
order:

as thou wast not the first of powers,
So art thou not the last; it cannot be:
Thou art not the beginning nor the end
            Mark well!
As Heaven and Earth are fairer, fairer far
Than Chaos and blank Darkness, though once chiefs;
And as we show beyond that Heaven and Earth
In form and shape compact and beautiful,
In will, in action free, companionship,
And thousand other signs of purer life;
So on our heels a fresh perfection treads,
A power more strong in beauty, born of us
And fated to excel us, as we pass
In glory that old Darkness.[11]

But if Shelley had to wait for time to remove tyranny and oppression, he could at least expose their evils in the meantime. And his poems abound in eloquent appeals for individual liberty and equality, far surpassing even the optimistic eloquence of the American Declaration of Independence. His greater works are poised between exposures of present tyranny and outlines of ideal society. In 'The Revolt of Islam', for example, he depicts with spine-chilling horror the effects of slaughter and plague, where the *corpses stare with horny eyes* among the *heaps of hearthless walls* and *black rafters*. But in the same poem there is an ecstatic vision of a new, free life:

> *O Love, who to the hearts of wandering men*
> *Art as the calm to Ocean's weary waves!*
> *Justice, or Truth, or Joy! those only can*
> *From slavery and religion's labyrinth caves*
> *Guide us . . .*
> *To feel the peace of self-contentment's lot,*
> *To own all sympathies, and outrage none . . .*
> *To live, as if to love and live were one,—*
> *This is not faith or law, nor those who bow*
> *To thrones on Heaven or Earth, such destiny may know.*[12]

In *Hellas*, too, before the vision of a new and better world, there is an explicit condemnation of present oppression, and a vivid evocation of a death-ridden tyranny, where *'The exhalations and the thirsty winds Are sick with blood'.*[13]

Nor was Shelley content to depict only distant or fictitious tyrannies. Poems such as 'England in 1819', 'Lines written during the Castlereagh Administration', 'Song to the Men of England', 'Similes for Two Political Characters of 1819', and 'A New National Anthem', all leave the reader in no doubt as to his views on the repression of liberty in his day—though it should be pointed out that Shelley was safely in Italy when he wrote them and that they were not published until many years after his death. But Shelley's sentiments about tyranny were by no means unknown to his contemporaries; if they had any doubts about his feelings and his belief in the eventual overthrow of despots, they had only to read his sonnet 'Ozymandias', published in 1818 by his friend Leigh Hunt, where the echoing emptiness reveals the hollow sham of the tyrant's power:

> *'My name is Ozymandias, king of kings:*
> *Look on my works, ye Mighty, and despair!'*

Nothing beside remains. Round the decay
Of that colossal wreck, boundless and bare
The lone and level sands stretch far away.

[1] Edmund Burke *Speeches and Letters on American Affairs* (Dent, 1955) p. 139   [2] William Blake 'America, a Prophecy' Plate 3, 8–10; 12   [3] *ibid.* Plate 6, 6–8; 10   [4] 'The Revolt of Islam' Canto XI, XXII (1–4); XXIII; XXIV (8)   [5] K.L. p. 273   [6] 'Queen Mab' III, 88–99   [7] 'The Revolt of Islam' Canto II, IV (4–5)   [8] *The Cenci* Act I, scene I, 100–2   [9] 'Queen Mab' II, 199–210   [10] *Hellas* 1084–89   [11] 'Hyperion' Book II, 188–90; 205–15   [12] 'The Revolt of Islam' Canto VIII, XI (1–5); XII (1–2, 7–9)   [13] *Hellas* 430–31

6

The Spirit of Romanticism

The word 'Romantic' has come to be applied to writings, paintings and music of a particular kind created in the later part of the eighteenth century, and the early nineteenth. It has various imprecise definitions, which are usually as generalized as those applied to the art of the first half of the eighteenth century, often called 'Classical' or 'Augustan'.

Both these latter terms came into use because the writers of this period were much influenced by ancient poets such as Virgil, Homer, Horace, Ovid, Pindar and Plutarch. These they regarded as exhibiting qualities so desirable that to emulate them would be to create literary works outstanding in form and content.

The same period, roughly the first half of the eighteenth century in England, was known as the 'Augustan Age', because, centuries before, there had been a period of great literary excellence in Rome under the Emperor Augustus (27 B.C.–A.D. 14) and because it was hoped to produce a similarly golden era in the English literary sphere.

'Romanticism' is usually taken to mean the reaction against the Classical movement which led to a new interest in individual feelings, a leaning away from the Augustan delight in reason to a new passion for mystery and the supernatural, a reaction against materialism and the recognition of the importance of the imagination. In this chapter we shall examine this shift of emphasis in some detail, particularly, of course, as it affected Keats and Shelley.

*　　　*　　　*

In the later seventeenth century, when the internal strife that had torn Britain apart during the Civil War and the Monmouth uprising seemed to be over, and the Settlement of 1688 had established William and Mary on the throne, a sense of relief enveloped the country. To be peaceful and secure was the general wish, and order and good sense were the desired qualities of life after the struggles and turmoil of the previous half-century.

At the same time, scientists such as Sir Isaac Newton were revealing, in works such as his *Philosophiae Naturalis Principia Mathematica*, published in 1687, that the universe was governed by recognizable laws. Man seemed to be part of an ordered system which could be followed and understood by observation interpreted by reason. The new, settled security of the nation seemed to the poet, Pope, to be reflected in the universe:

> *And if each system in gradation roll,*
> *Alike essential to th'amazing whole;*
> *The least confusion but in one, not all*
> *That system only, but the whole must fall.*[1]

Society was a miniature universe, where reason and rules of right conduct could ensure peace and harmony.

14. *Newton* by William Blake. Blake, as a Romantic, felt that Newton represented the kind of tightly logical scientific thought which left no room for inspired imaginings. Consequently, he depicts Newton as earthbound, with his eyes riveted earthwards, and almost on all fours like an animal. (Tate Gallery, London)

Models for such conduct—as also for good writing—could be found in the works of ancient poets, which were reaching a rapidly increasing public. The mercantile middle classes were growing in numbers, and sent their sons to be educated in grammar schools which usually adhered to a rigidly classical curriculum. For those whose education was lacking, translations of the best ancient Greek and Roman writings proliferated. Dryden, the most eminent writer at the end of the seventeenth century, had translated the whole of Virgil, and sections of Ovid, Homer, Horace, and Juvenal. And in his *Essay of Dramatick Poesie*, published in 1668, where Dryden had depicted four friends discussing drama, the 'rules' laid down by ancient writers, particularly Aristotle and Horace, are frequently cited. When Pope published his 'Essay on Criticism' in 1711, he put forward a similar view; the art of poetry discovered by ancient writers was *'Nature still, but Nature methodiz'd'* by rules. A detailed knowledge of the classics is therefore necessary in order to evaluate good writing:

> *You then whose judgement the right course would steer,*
> *Know well each ANCIENT's proper character;*
> *His fable, subject, scope in ev'ry page;*
> *Religion, country, genius of his age:*
> *Without all these at once before your eyes,*
> *Cavil you may, but never criticize . . .*
> *Learn hence for ancient rules a just esteem;*
> *To copy Nature is to copy them.*[2]

'*Copying Nature*' did not mean wild, disordered behaviour; on the contrary, the phrase relies on the belief that all men have common experience and feelings which allow for standards of decency and good taste to be 'natural' among civilized men. Strange, eccentric behaviour or erratic passions were not therefore the proper subject of literature, which, to have any value, should reflect the interests of and appeal to the tastes of society in general. If one were in doubt as to what good taste should be, one could find out from publications such as *The Spectator*, a periodical issued by Richard Steele and Joseph Addison from 1711-2, and later published in collected form. Here, the reader could be instructed in morality or manners, or discover what he should be thinking about literature. Such conformity was not considered hypocrisy; on the contrary, as long as one obeyed one's conscience in higher matters, such as religion, to do what society expected in matters of taste was an obligation. Writing to his son in 1748, Lord Chesterfield, whose sense of propriety was legendary, made the distinction very plain:

> *I need not, I believe, advise you to adapt your conversation to*
> *the people you are conversing with; for I suppose you would*
> *not, without this caution, have talked upon the same subject*
> *and in the same manner to a Minister of State, a Bishop, a*

philosopher, a Captain, and a woman. A man of the world must, like a chameleon, be able to take every different line, which is by no means a criminal or abject, but a necessary complaisance, for it relates only to manners and not to morals.[3]

A man of the world, Lord Chesterfield felt, should be dignified, and yet fashionable:

There is a certain dignity of manners absolutely necessary . . . Horse-play, romping, frequent and loud fits of laughter . . . compose at most a merry fellow; and a merry fellow was never yet a respectable man.[4] *. . . I should be sorry you were an egregious fop; but I protest that, of the two, I would rather have you a fop than a sloven.*[5] *. . . Your dancing master is at this time the man in all Europe of the greatest importance to you. You must dance well, in order to sit, stand and walk well; and you must do all these well, in order to please.*[6]

15. *Nebuchadnezzar* by William Blake. Nebuchadnezzar, the Bible tells us, gloated in his own power and was punished by being made to live like an animal. So Blake sees the man who glories in commercial prosperity; he is bestial, degraded—one stage nearer the earth than Newton. (Tate Gallery, London)

Such advice could only be given in a world where men believed they knew exactly what was required of a cultured man in dress, taste, manners and morals—and further, that such requirements could be taught. That such was the belief can be deduced from the amount of didactic (that is, deliberately instructive) poetry to be found in the early eighteenth century, and especially from the proliferation of satire. Satire sets out to teach good behaviour by ridiculing the bad, and the late seventeenth and early eighteenth century abounds in satirical verse, such as Dryden's 'Absalom and Achitophel' and Pope's 'Dunciad', and satirical prose, such as Swift's *Gulliver's Travels*. The common use of heroic couplets (two lines, rhyming together, and forming a unit) often in the form of an epigram—that is, a witty, almost proverbial, thought or saying—and reinforced by the use of contrast, was the perfect medium for verse which frequently addresses the reader in the tone of dictatorial teacher to ignorant pupil:

> *A little learning is a dangerous Thing;*
> *Drink deep, or taste not the Pierian Spring;*[7]
> *... Fear not the Anger of the Wise to raise;*
> *Those best can bear reproof, who merit Praise.*[8]

One could obviously find numerous exceptions, but, in general, the eighteenth-century middle-class man of the world liked a settled, ordered society, where rules of conduct were clearly defined and where Britain's expanding empire could remind him, optimistically, of the Roman Empire at its Augustan best. In the field of literary criticism, too, such virtues were reinforced by perhaps the greatest eighteenth-century Augustan, Dr Samuel Johnson. In his article outlining his plan for a dictionary of the English language, Johnson makes it clear that general truths and clear instruction are virtues in the field of words as much as in daily social activities:

> *the words and phrases used in the general intercourse of life, or found in the works of those whom we commonly style polite writers, be selected, without including the terms of particular professions. . . . It is not enough that a dictionary delights the critic, unless at the same time it instructs the learner.*

'The general *intercourse of life*' sums up what Dr Johnson and many of his contemporaries regarded as the proper subject of literature. Ideas too individual, imaginations too strange, thoughts too uncommon, were not likely to give pleasure. It is '*uniformity of sentiment*', he tells us,

> *which enables us to conceive and to excite the pains and the pleasures of other minds.*

To be too precise is to lose '*the grandeur of generality*' while to strive for new ideas is futile: everything worth saying has already been said:

> *Those writers who lay on the watch for novelty could have little hope of greatness; for great things cannot have escaped former observation.*

Throughout the eighteenth century, of course, there were writers who did not at all adhere to the classical rules and whose writings reveal much individual sensibility. The novel, being a form unknown to the classical world, could not be modelled on ancient rules, and 'picaresque' novels, such as Defoe's *Moll Flanders*, had concentrated on the highly individual adventures of a roguish hero or 'picaro'. And even within the classical framework, the best writers brought freshness and vitality to their work. But, in spite of these exceptions, there was a tendency for *'the grandeur of generality'* to become the staleness of generalization. A new beginning was clearly called for. Towards the end of the eighteenth century, then, began the breakaway from Classicism which we know as the Romantic movement.

It was by no means a movement confined to literature alone. As we shall see in Chapter 11, music and painting experienced similar changes. The taste for order and formality in the sphere of gardening gave way first to landscape gardening, then to delight in the picturesque, and then to pleasure in wild, 'sublime' nature, as we shall see in Chapter 8. The stress on the importance of reason and good sense diminished, and horror stories, with tales of dreams and the supernatural, became almost universally popular. In almost every sphere of existence, a movement away from classical order to romantic freedom could be traced.

What were the causes of this gradual change? Obviously they were many, and no one reason can be given precedence over any other. An obvious, yet probably viable, explanation, is that people were simply bored with a century of settled formality and carefully defined good taste. The deliciously ridiculous thrill of a supernatural horror story or the delightfully scandalous eccentricities of a Lord Byron were a welcome relief from the measured tones of a Dr Johnson or the never-failing propriety of a Lord Chesterfield. At a deeper level, there was, as we have seen in the three previous chapters, a growing uneasiness with the state of society, both in the political and social spheres. An ever-increasing impatience with a materialistic society, and an urgent insistence on the spiritual values, led many men to reject society's standard values and to concentrate on eternal truth as perceived through individual experience.

It is impossible to say precisely where and when the first glimmerings of the Romantic movement began. Certainly Jean Jacques Rousseau (1712–78) was one of the earliest and most important influences. As we have already seen, his writings were to have a radical effect on eighteenth-century political reformists. In his *Confessions*, published after his death, he gave vividly individual recollections of personal events; there was no attempt here at generality—his unique thoughts in particularized circumstances were his subject. Nor did Rousseau praise formal, ordered society; on the contrary, it was society, he felt, which was responsible for evil. Man in a natural environment would be virtuous.

Writings such as this were calculated to question the whole Augustan way of life. At the same time, political tremors were running through society which ensured that this previous way of life was to be forcibly changed. In 1776, we saw in the previous chapter, the American colonists had issued their Declaration of Independence, and embarked on a successful war to establish their freedom from Britain, showing that it was now possible to break away from a traditional, paternalistic order, and to dare to tread new paths. The American Dream had begun, and the pioneering spirit which set out to conquer this vast new land spread its infectious optimism across the sea, with tales from such men as the traveller Birkbeck of enormous tracts of land to be had for the taking. Keats' own brother George was one of those who caught the infection.

Only six years after the ending of the American War of Independence came the French Revolution. Here again, ideals of individual freedom, of upsetting established orders, of liberty after restraint, were forcibly brought before the minds of all Europe. Then the rise of Napoleon suggested to many that a privileged birth was not necessary to achieve greatness and power; individual talent could overcome all obstacles.

Simultaneously, the struggle against slavery, described in the previous chapter, brought to men's minds a new concept of the dignity and importance of the individual, while the struggles of the Irish Catholics highlighted the question of liberty of conscience.

In all these ways, then, a new climate of opinion was gradually being created in which a radically different approach to English poetry—the Romantic approach—could flourish. In 1798 appeared the first clearly Romantic book of English poetry—*Lyrical Ballads*. This contained poems by Wordsworth and Coleridge, and broke away entirely from the traditional artificial poetry of the Augustan Age. Wordsworth's poems were simple, naturally told stories of simple natural individuals, while Coleridge's major contribution, *The Rime of the Ancient Mariner*, startlingly exhibited the Romantic interest in visions and the supernatural. When the second edition of the poems appeared in 1800, Wordsworth had written a Preface, in which he registered his intention to produce *'a class of poetry . . . well adapted to interest mankind permanently'*. He recognized that his poems and Coleridge's are:

> *so materially different from those upon which general approbation is at present bestowed.*

In this new volume of poetry, feelings and emotions are given a new importance; it is feeling expressed in the poems which:

> *gives importance to the action and situation, and not the action and situation to the feeling.*

This insistence on the importance of feeling, together with the intense interest in the world of Nature (see Chapter 8), are two aspects of Romanticism clearly seen in Wordsworth. A third is the feeling, developed further by Keats, that all experiences are proper subjects for poetry, which, Wordsworth wrote, is *'the first and last of all knowledge'*.

Coleridge's poem, *The Ancient Mariner*, clearly exhibited two further aspects of Romanticism. One is the interest in the man cast out of society, the eccentric, the scapegoat; the other is the interest in the supernatural. Both these interests, of course, went entirely against the Augustan interest in man as a member of society, and in reasonable good sense. Coleridge's ancient mariner kills an albatross, and is cursed. The ship falls under a strange spell, and all the crew except the ancient mariner die. The strange visions the mariner sees, the spirits who guide the ship, the fate laid upon the mariner—all these are outside the normal range of Augustan interests.

The validity of individual experiences; the importance of the imagination; the belief that all of life is the proper subject for poetry; the interest in dreams and the supernatural—all these aspects of Romanticism are important to Shelley, and are at the very heart of Keats' philosophy of poetry.

Writing to Bailey in November, 1817, Keats stresses that, in his view:

> *at the imagination seizes as Beauty must be truth—*
> *nether it existed before or not . . . The Imagination may be*
> *compared to Adam's dream*—he awoke and found it truth—*
> *I have never yet been able to perceive how anything can be*
> *known for truth by consequitive [consecutive] reasoning . . .*
> *O for a Life of sensations rather than of Thoughts.*[9]

Lord Byron, in his *Childe Harold's Pilgrimage*, expressed the same idea. The reality of the mind and imagination is more real than everyday physical life:

> *'Tis to create, and in creating live*
> *A being more intense, that we endow*
> *With form our fancy, gaining as we give*
> *The life we image . . .*
> *What am I? Nothing: but not so art thou,*
> *Soul of my thought!*[10]

Keats explored this idea further in 'Ode on a Grecian Urn', where he feels that the existence depicted by the artist has a reality more vital than his own; moreover, it will last eternally:

> *Heard melodies are sweet, but those unheard*
> *Are sweeter; therefore ye soft pipes, play on;*
> *Not to the sensual ear, but, more endear'd*
> *Pipe to the spirit ditties of no tone:*
> *Fair youth, beneath the trees, thou canst not leave*
> *Thy song, nor ever can those trees be bare.*

He sees this essential reality in the beauty of the urn, which teaches man that:

> *Beauty is truth, truth beauty.*

The eighteenth-century interest in order, certainty and reason was also rejected by Keats, who saw it, not as a sign of intellectual maturity but of spiritual littleness: writing to his brothers in December, 1817, he reveals how it suddenly struck him:

> *what quality went to form a Man of Achievement, especially*
> *in Literature, and which Shakespeare possessed so enormously*
> *— I mean Negative Capability, that is, when a man is capable*
> *of being in uncertainties, mysteries, doubts without any irritable*
> *reaching after fact and reason.*[11]

---

* Adam in Milton's *Paradise Lost* dreamt of the creation of Eve, and, awakening, found that she really existed.

A poem which perfectly illustrates Keats' belief in the reality of imagination, and his willingness to be in uncertainties, is 'Ode to a Nightingale'. (It also, of course, illustrates other important features of his poetry, such as his delight in nature; his despair at the miseries of life; and his interest in the rich sensuousness of words, revealed through stylistic devices such as assonance and alliteration.)

In this poem, Keats wonders how we could escape from the grief of the world to reach the happiness of the nightingale. The only valid way, he feels, is through imagination. By entering into his imagination, he can experience the eternal joys and sorrows created and calmed by the song of the nightingale through countless ages. At last he returns to reality—but is it reality? Now the imagination has become truth; he no longer knows whether he is awake or asleep. Conscious, logical thought is meaningless in the face of this experience.

It is a theme which Keats explores over and over again. As a Romantic poet, he feels the world of dreams is as real as the world of consecutive thought—more real in fact—and Keats, like Adam, 'awoke and found it truth'. In 'Endymion', the hero dreams of meeting Cynthia—yet when he awakes, he does not know which is reality, which dream:

> And then I fell asleep. Ah, can I tell
> The enchantment that afterwards befel?
> Yet was it but a dream: yet such a dream
> That never tongue, although it overteem
> With mellow utterance, like a cavern spring,
> Could figure out and to conception bring
> All I beheld and felt.[12]

And as he describes the vision which he 'dreamt', his sister Peona sums up the mysticism of the experience:

> 'Endymion, how strange!
> Dream within dream!'[13]

But it is no dream—or, if it is, it is intensely real.

The same is true of two experiences in 'Lamia'. The god Hermes pursues a nymph, who is protected by invisibility; he is granted his wish of seeing her, and:

> It was no dream; or say a dream it was,
> Real are the dreams of Gods, and smoothly pass
> Their pleasures in a long immortal dream.[14]

In the same poem, Lycius is *'saved'* by the philosopher Apollonius, who, with his cool reasoning, perceives the falseness of the dream-world in which Lamia has entangled Lycius. But:

> *Philosophy will clip an angel's wings,*
> *Conquer all mysteries by rule and line . . .*
> *Unweave a rainbow,*[15]

and deprived of his dream, which to him was reality, Lycius is deprived of life. Apollonius represents *'consecutive reasoning'*—what Wordsworth, writing in 1798, had called *'Our meddling intellect'* which, far from bringing truth, *'mis-shapes the beauteous form of things.'* To Lycius, the *'beauteous form'* of Lamia was real enough.

In 'The Eve of St Agnes' too, reality and dream are intertwined for Madeline, when Porphyro comes to her:

> *Shaded was her dream*
> *By the dusk curtains:—'twas a midnight charm*
> *Impossible to melt as iced stream. . . .*
> *Her eyes were open, but she still beheld*
> *Now wide awake, the vision of her sleep. . . .*
> *Into her dream he melted, as the rose*
> *Blendeth its odour with the violet.*[16]

And in 'Hyperion', too, Apollo finds that Mnemosyne, formerly seen in dreams, has become reality:

> *'Sure I have heard those vestments sweeping o'er*
> *The fallen leaves, when I have sat alone*
> *In cool mid-forest . . .*
> *Goddess! I have beheld those eyes before,*
> *And their eternal calm, and all that face,*
> *Or I have dreamed.'—'Yes,' said the supreme shape,*
> *'Thou hast dream'd of me . . .*
> *The watcher of thy sleep and hours of life.'*[17]

In all these poems Keats shows how imagination can be more real—that is, more vital and important—than anything conveyed by logical thought. It is a central theme of perhaps his most important poem, 'The Fall of Hyperion', where it is combined with another Romantic idea—the belief that one's own intensely personal experiences are a proper subject for poetry. For 'The Fall of Hyperion' explores Keats' own strivings to achieve poetic greatness.

It is set in the framework of a vision, introduced by a declaration of the importance of imagination to the poet:

For Poesy alone can tell her dreams—
With the fine spell of words alone can save
Imagination from the sable charm
And dumb enchantment . . .
. . . every man whose soul is not a clod
Hath visions, and would speak, if he had lov'd
And been well nurtured in his mother Tongue.
Whether the dream now purposed to rehearse
Be poet's or fanatic's will be known
When this warm scribe, my hand, is in the grave.[18]

The aspiring poet then dreams of a banquet—and here we see the Romantic delight in sensation. Sight, touch, taste, smell and sound are all explored and enjoyed—as they are in most of Keats' poems. But here their significance is greater; he describes how he drank from *'a cool vessel of transparent juice'*, and in this symbolic act of giving himself up to a life of sensation, he is transported to the threshold of poetic excellence (here symbolized as a temple, whose steps he must ascend). The numbness which seizes him and threatens to overwhelm him is what he describes elsewhere as *'Lethe'* and as *'The feel of not to feel it'*—that is, the deadening of sensation, which would be death to the true Romantic poet.

Here, as we saw in Chapter 4, he learns that the true poet must feel for the miseries of others. The belief that the true poet experiences intense sympathetic suffering for his fellow man is an essential ingredient of Romanticism, and, of course, is closely linked to the emphasis on imagination, for without imagination a total sympathy is impossible. From their sense of disillusionment with society and their deep melancholy, the Romantic writers saw that man's only hope of salvation lay in a deeper humanity. Keats, writing to his brother George, comments that:

Very few men have ever arrived at a complete disinterestedness of Mind: very few have been influenced by a pure desire of the benefit of others . . . as Wordsworth says, 'we have all one human heart.'[19]

The same stress on the importance of humanity had been made by the poet Blake, who asked:

Can I see another's woe
And not be in sorrow too?
Can I see another's grief
And not seek for kind relief?[20]

It was just such a feeling for fellow man which had made Wordsworth, looking at joyful Nature, grieve for *'What man has made of
man'*. It was a similar sensation which made Shelley, writing in the
Preface to 'Alastor', comment that:

> *Those who love not their fellow beings live unfruitful lives, and
> prepare for their old age a miserable grave.*

Sensitivity to others' sufferings was vitally important, then; but,
as we have seen, the Romantic poet was also intensely conscious of
the importance of individual experience. So much so, that, like the
Gothic horror novels (see Chapter 7) which had laid stress on
extraordinary adventures and strange experiences, the Romantic
poets were interested in the *uniqueness* of an individual's situation.
As we saw when discussing Coleridge's *The Ancient Mariner*, part
of the Romanticism of the poem lies in the view of the mariner as an
outcast, experiencing sufferings which no other man had ever undergone. It was a theme dear to the Romantic hearts. Common in
Romantic poetry is the exiled hero, the man misunderstood by
society, or too great for it, who suffers because he cannot or will not
conform to its petty standards. Like Byron's Childe Harold, such
a man:

> *knew himself the most unfit
> Of men to herd with Man; with whom he held
> Little in common; untaught to submit
> His thoughts to others, though his soul was quell'd
> In youth by his own thought; still uncompell'd,
> He would not yield dominion of his mind
> To spirits against whom his own rebell'd;
> Proud though in desolation; which could find
> A life within itself, to breathe without mankind.*[21]

Another example of such a man is the Faust of the German poet
Goethe; he has fully explored the avenues of human knowledge,
and is bored with it all. The only untrodden path is that of magic,
and he follows it with a sense that it will put him above and beyond
common humanity, making him a kind of god.

Like Faust, the hero of Byron's play, *Manfred*, also chooses magic
as his way to godlike knowledge. Manfred is trebly isolated from
the rest of mankind—by living high up in the Alps; by carrying a
deadly secret of guilt (strongly hinted at as being incest); and by
seeking to learn more of the universe than any other man, by magic.

16. *Manfred on the Jungfrau* by Ford Madox Brown. Ford Madox Brown, like many of the Pre-Raphaelite artists, took his inspiration from events in literature. Here, Byron's *Manfred* also provides the artist with a chance to portray mountainous scenery and medieval costume, both of which were of interest to Romantic writers. (City Art Gallery, Manchester)

Keats' heroes are not outcasts in this strange, self-inflicted way; and yet often his poems show us an individual isolated from the rest of society by a unique experience. Endymion loves a goddess and cannot rest amongst his own people; Porphyro loves the daughter of an enemy family; Isabella broods helplessly over her murdered love; the knight-at-arms in 'La Belle Dame sans Merci' is *'alone'* on the edge of the lake and no other living man shares his experience;

and in 'The Fall of Hyperion', the poet undergoes a unique mystical experience.

Shelley, who of course personified the Romantic outcast in his own experiences, also examines this sense of isolation. His poem 'Alastor', subtitled 'The Spirit of Solitude', traces the story of an individual unhappily isolated. Having studied all knowledge deeply, he is still unsatisfied, and at last realizes that he desires a companion, and his mind seeks *an intelligence similar to itself*. Interestingly, Shelley explores here, like Keats, the idea of the importance of dreams, for it is in a dream that the young poet of the story sees, loves and enjoys, like Keats' Endymion, the perfect woman. But unlike Endymion, Shelley's poet does not find her in reality, and his isolation leads to his death.

It was exactly this theme which was to be at the centre of Mary Shelley's novel, *Frankenstein*, which explores many of the concepts of Romanticism. Like Faust, like Manfred, Frankenstein's egotism is his undoing. He meddles with forces beyond his control, and creates a *'monster'*. Yet this *'monster'* is only physically ugly; spiritually he is fine, until denied association with other beings. When he finds that he is an outcast, he seeks, like the poet in 'Alastor', a single companion. It is only when he is denied this comfort that his misery turns to hatred for mankind:

> *'Shall each man,' cried he, 'find a wife for his bosom, and each beast have his mate, and I be alone? I had feelings of affection, and they were requited by detestation and scorn . . . Man, you shall repent of the injuries you inflict.'*

Shelley's isolated heroes are usually isolated in this way, failing to fit into the world in which they find themselves, though intrinsically endowed with noble qualities—as Shelley saw himself, of course. Such is true of Laon and Cythna in 'The Revolt of Islam', of Beatrice in *The Cenci*, and, most notably, of Prometheus.

We have mentioned that Shelley, like Keats, explores the Romantic idea of imagination, dreams, visions. For Shelley, as we saw in Chapter 3, the most significant of these was his vision of a new world, which he saw at times as an inevitable reality in the future, and at times as merely a hope in his imagination. Even at his most despondent, however, this vision of a new society, a *'brighter Hellas'*, was intensely real to him, while even the most cursory reading of his poetry will show that 'reality' in the normal sense of the word was of minimal importance. The vision of Cythna, imprisoned in a cave beneath the sea, fed by *'a sea-eagle'*; the setting and the action of *Prometheus Unbound*—where, for example, the god describes how:

> *shapeless sights come wandering by,*
> *The ghastly people of the realm of dream,*
> *Mocking me: and the Earthquake-fiends are charged*
> *To wrench the rivets from my quivering wounds*
> *When the rocks split and close again behind;* [22]

or the description of the cave of the Witch of Atlas where lay hidden:

> *sounds of air . . .*
> *Folded in cells of crystal silence there; . . .*
> *And there lay visions swift, and sweet, and quaint,*
> *Each in its thin sheath, like a chrysalis.* [23]

—these are not 'real' in the sense of observable fact; but they may become intensely real if seized by the imagination.

And it is this feeling that the life of the imagination is as real and vital as the actual world, and perhaps more fulfilling, which sets the Romantic English poet aside from his Augustan forebears. Thomas Hobbes, the seventeenth-century philosopher whose work *Leviathan* influenced eighteenth-century thought, wrote that *'a great fancy is one kind of madness'*. But to Keats and other Romantic poets, *'a great fancy'* was the key to essential reality: *'What the imagination seizes as Beauty must be truth.'*

[1] Alexander Pope 'An Essay on Man' Epistle I, 247–50 [2] Alexander Pope 'Essay on Criticism' 119–23; 139–40 [3] Lord Chesterfield *Letters of Lord Chesterfield to His Son and Others* (Dent, 1935) p. 78 [4] *ibid.* p. 110 [5] *ibid.* p. 120 [6] *ibid.* p. 207 [7] Alexander Pope 'Essay on Criticism' 215–16 [8] *ibid.* 582–3 [9] K.L. p. 75 [10] Lord Byron *Childe Harold's Pilgrimage* Canto III, VI [11] K.L. p. 81 [12] 'Endymion' Book I, 572–8; [13] *ibid.* 632–3 [14] 'Lamia' Part I, 126–8 [15] *ibid.* Part II, 234–5; 237 [16] 'The Eve of St Agnes' XXXII (2–4); XXXIV (1–2); XXXVI (5–6) [17] 'Hyperion' Book III, 53–5; 59–62; 72 [18] 'The Fall of Hyperion' 8–11; 13–18 [19] K.L. p. 272–3 [20] William Blake *Songs of Innocence* ('On Another's Sorrow') [21] as 10, Canto III, XII [22] *Prometheus Unbound* Act I, 36–40 [23] 'The Witch of Atlas' 154–7; 161–2

7

The Interest in Medievalism

The aspect of the English Romantic movement which perhaps penetrated most deeply into everyday life was the renewed interest in all things medieval. The fashion for 'Gothic', as it was termed, permeated every aspect of existence, and—as it lingered on well into the reign of Victoria, giving rise to the great Gothic Revival—is still in evidence today; many a parish church, village school, or railway station, inherited from our Victorian forebears, is built in sham medieval style, with triple-arched windows, complete with tracery, buttresses and battlements.

This delight in the past seems to have gained momentum as the mechanization and industrialization of life increased. As we saw in Chapter 4, commerce and materialism seemed to erode worthwhile values; it is not surprising, therefore, that there was great interest in a fashion which combined pure escapism with an attempt to revive what was seen as the nobler life of a past age. In the Gothic era, men saw, probably quite falsely, a finer civilization, and attempted to recreate it by surrounding themselves with reproductions of past splendour.

It was in the form of pseudo-medieval buildings that the eighteenth-century taste for Gothic was most spectacularly indulged. In 1749, Sir Horace Walpole began the task of turning his house at Strawberry Hill, Twickenham, into a mock medieval castle. So successful was the idea that Walpole was plagued with visitors, and even printed admission tickets. Some fifty years later the architect James Wyatt was to carry out the same sort of scheme on a far more extravagant scale for the millionaire James Beckford; his Gothic alterations to Fonthill Abbey were, quite literally, out of all proportion, and it was not really surprising when the 84 m high tower, dominating the 122 m long wings of the house, crashed to the ground, owing to weak foundations.

Not everyone could afford, or wanted to afford, such extraordinary examples of mock-medievalism. But many indulged their interest in the new fashion by discovering ruins in their grounds,

or building them when they could not be discovered, as Sir Kenneth Clarke describes in *The Gothic Revival*:

> *At first they were classical, since they were chiefly inspired by Italian landscape . . . . But there were reasons why fashionable taste came to prefer Gothic: for one thing authentic ruins were often as effective as sham ones and cost nothing to erect; and in England practically all the authentic ruins are medieval. Then Gothic was the fashionable melancholy . . .*

17. The Gothic Gallery, Strawberry Hill. Horace Walpole's extravagant mansion shows how the taste for medieval ornamentation could be carried to the ultimate extreme. (A. F. Kersting, London)

Those who already had a castle to hand, as it were, often entered happily into the fashion. James Wyatt, who had had such extravagant architectural fun with Fonthill, later set to work on Belvoir Castle in Leicestershire. It had once been a fortress, but had been rebuilt in the seventeenth century. Wyatt turned it back into a fortress, in appearance at least, with a tower and turrets. Inside, however, there was no medieval discomfort; the house was elegantly furnished in Regency style, with a decided French rococo influence. Such a compromise—medieval outside, contemporary elegance inside—characterized much of the 'gothicizing' of the period, such as the vastly expensive alterations at Windsor Castle.

But, if one wanted to follow the Gothic fashion with determined thoroughness, and be medieval in tone inside as well as outside the house, then there was no difficulty. On the contrary, it would have been possible to be medieval in style in almost every item of household equipment. Chippendale was producing chairs in the Gothic style in the mid-eighteenth century, and Robert Adams designed in the same fashion. Wallpaper with medieval motifs was available. Panels of pseudo-medieval stained glass were designed.

The pointed arch with ornamental tracery, so common in fourteenth- and fifteenth-century English church architecture, was reproduced everywhere—on the backs of chairs, the bases of vases, the fronts of cabinets, or in purely decorative panels. Everything from clocks to candlesticks, fans to fish-slices, might be covered with Gothic tracery and medieval ornamentation.

One reason for the widespread and wholehearted interest in Gothic seems to have been a taste for the strange, the bizarre and the outlandish, developed as a reaction not only against growing industrialization, but also against the rationality and 'good taste' of the Augustan period, which was beginning to seem stale and restricting. In this connection, things medieval were not the only vogue; a taste for the Oriental was also fashionable. Here, as with Gothic, it was possible to indulge one's fancy for the East in the external design of one's house, or in internal decoration, or, as in the case of the Prince Regent, in both.

The Royal Pavilion at Brighton—gradually transformed from a farmhouse to a palace between 1787 and 1822 for the Prince Regent, later George IV—is overpowering in its desire to imitate the Orient. The massive swelling domes outside seem paradoxically insignificant when one is actually inside, and dominated by the vast, brooding dragons, the towering pagodas, the bulging water-lily lights that decorate the principal rooms.

Bamboo abounds—not real bamboo, but fine imitations in carved wood or cast iron. Oriental statues and vases fill up every vacant corner. Even in the kitchen, the dream of the East continues, and four gigantic cast-iron and copper palm-trees shoot from floor to ceiling. It is interesting to note that among many who shared the

Prince Regent's taste for the wonders of the East was Beckford, author of the oriental tale, *Vathek*, in which the palace of the Caliph is described in terms that would equally suit the Royal Pavilion:

> *The palace named 'The Delight of the Eyes' . . . was one of entire enchantment. Rarities, collected from every corner of the earth, were there found in such profusion as to dazzle and confound, but for the order in which they were arranged. . . . Vathek omitted nothing in this palace that might gratify the curiosity of those who resorted to it, although he was not able to satisfy his own; for of all men, he was the most curious.*

The Prince Regent and Beckford had this in common, that, at Brighton, as at Fonthill, the taste for the exotic became indecently extravagant and financially scandalous.

But the excesses of Fonthill and the Royal Pavilion serve to show the intense delight, the thrill of excitement, that such bizarre creations could arouse. Inevitably, the tastes which the rich indulged so ostentatiously became the tastes, less spectacularly, of the general public, and the weird, the strange, the exotic became commonplaces of public entertainment. In novels, poems and plays, the taste for medievalism was constantly indulged.

18. The Banqueting Room at The Royal Pavilion, Brighton, an aquatint from *Views of the Royal Pavilion 1820–5* by John Nash. The massive overhanging leaves and dragons, the ornamental vases and Chinese murals all combine to give this enormous room the Eastern flavour which the Prince Regent required. (John R. Freeman, London)

The work which is generally considered the forerunner of the vogue for the 'Gothic horror' novel in Britain is Horace Walpole's *The Castle of Otranto*, published in 1765, ostensibly as a translation of a medieval tale. There had already been 'novels of sentiment', such as Richardson's *Pamela* (published 1740–1) and *Clarissa Harlowe* (published 1747–8) in which the heroines undergo imprisonment, degradation and privation, and suffer—or in Pamela's case nearly suffer—a fate worse than death. But in Walpole's story the innocent, suffering heroine and noble hero undergo their ordeals, not amidst civilized English countryside, but in a strange, gloomy, haunted castle. Walpole quite unashamedly makes use of the supernatural, which was to become a feature of Gothic novels, and wastes no time in introducing his readers to an element of mystery and horror.

On the first page of the novel, we read of an ancient and mystifying prophecy. On the second page we are plunged into horror:

> The servant . . . came running back breathless, in a frantic manner, his eyes staring, and foaming at the mouth. He said nothing but pointed to the court. The company were struck with terror and amazement . . . Manfred . . . went himself to get information of what occasioned this strange confusion . . . But what a sight for a father's eyes! He beheld his child dashed to pieces, and almost buried under an enormous helmet, an hundred times more large than any casque ever made for human being, and shaded with a proportionable quantity of black feather.

The description is so ludicrous that a 'willing suspension of disbelief' would be impossible—were it not for Walpole's careful distancing of the scene from eighteenth-century English reality. The scene is set in Italy—a strange and exciting country; and the period is some time in the mists of the medieval era. The Gothic element does not merely add an exciting air of mystery, it offers a convenient excuse for any incident which would appear too outlandish if set in contemporary society. In her clever satire on Gothic novels, *Northanger Abbey*, published posthumously in 1818, Jane Austen perceptively shows that credulity is helped by a deliberate distancing effect:

> Italy, Switzerland and the South of France, might be fruitful in horrors . . . Among the Alps and Pyrenees, perhaps, there were no such mixed characters. There, such as were not spotless as an angel, might have the disposition of a fiend. But in

England it was not so; among the English, she believed, in their hearts and habits, there was a general though unequal mixture of good and bad.

The Castle of Otranto immediately linked medieval castles with horror in the public mind. Otranto seems riddled with dark vaults, subterraneous passages, trap-doors and caverns—an environment which had such popular appeal and was so often recreated that Coleridge, writing in *Biographia Literaria* in 1817, complains of:

> *the ruined castles, the dungeons, the trap-doors, the skeletons, the flesh and blood ghosts, and the perpetual moonshine of a modern author.*[1]

The sneer at *'flesh and blood ghosts'* might well be taken to refer to the works of Ann Radcliffe, whose novels, especially *The Mysteries of Udolpho* (published in 1794) and *The Italian* (1797) were immediately popular. These tales do not take place in the distant past, but they are set among medieval castles and monasteries in France, Switzerland and Italy. Mrs Radcliffe makes use of all the horrors of the supernatural, without supernatural events actually occurring. In *The Mysteries of Udolpho*, for example, Dorothée, the housekeeper, indicates the bed in which her mistress died, and which is now covered by a black counterpane:

> *She had scarcely uttered these words, when the pall was more violently agitated than before; but Emily, somewhat ashamed of her terrors, stepped back to the bed, willing to be convinced that the wind only had occasioned her alarm; when, as she gazed within the curtains, the pall moved again, and, in the next moment, the apparition of a human countenance rose above it.*
>
> *Screaming with terror, they both fled.*

It is something of an anticlimax when we discover later that it was no apparition, but a *real* human countenance, that of a smuggler, concealed in the bed.

Similarly, the ghastly sight behind the black veil with which Mrs Radcliffe so delightfully terrorized poor Catherine in Jane Austen's *Northanger Abbey*:

> *'I know it must be a skeleton; I am sure it is Laurentina's skeleton'*—

turns out, tamely, to be a wax image made as a *'momento mori'*.

Nevertheless, there is nothing lame or disappointing about the settings of the novels. The castles are as medieval as the sternest critic could require:

> *The towers were united by a curtain, pierced and embattled also, below which appeared the pointed arch of an huge portcullis—*

and as ruined and gloomy as one could wish for:

> *Emily . . . looked fearfully on the almost roofless walls green with damps, and on the gothic points of the windows, where the ivy and the briony had long supplied the place of glass, and ran mantling among the broken capitals of some columns, that had once supported the roof. Barnardine stumbled . . . and his voice, as he uttered a sudden oath, was returned in hollow echoes.*

Nor are the sufferings of heroes and heroines in Gothic novels allowed to be slight. Imprisonment, rape, murder—often at the hands of perverted nuns or monks—such things are commonplace, especially in the novel by Matthew Gregory Lewis, immensely popular and widely condemned when published in 1796, which earned him his nickname 'Monk' Lewis.

Such novels might well be regarded today as sheer escapism. On the surface, they appear to have little to do with realism—though a closer reading often reveals perceptive description of scenery and a real attempt to portray shifts of feeling. Certainly they appeared to Jane Austen to be totally divorced from reality, and for that reason their immense popularity was suspect. The ludicrous scene in *Northanger Abbey*, in which Catherine struggles in the dark to discover the mysteries concealed in a black cabinet, only to find a laundry-bill, and the even more ludicrous suspicions she harbours concerning General Tilney's treatment of his wife, are grim warnings to young ladies too easily taken in by the pleasures of the circulating libraries* and it is the public taste which is being queried when Henry gently rebukes Catherine:

---

* Such libraries were the eighteenth-century equivalent of our modern Public Libraries; but in those days a membership fee was charged, and only subscribers could borrow books. The growth of such libraries obviously encouraged the growth of the reading public, which was in any case expanding as the numbers of leisured middle-class wives and daughters increased, and such ladies were a ready market for the many novels published at this time.

Consult your own understanding, your own sense of the probable, your own observation of what is passing around you . . . what ideas have you been admitting?

But if the taste for medievalism went hand in hand with the unbelievable in the Gothic horror novel, in other areas of literature it fostered a growing interest in realism. There was a growing passion for 'true' medievalism, not in the fictional Gothic but in historical fact (even if the history was not always very carefully investigated). Many writers saw medieval life as offering an ideal of nobility and harmony, where feudal ties linked men together in a way which was impossible in their contemporary, factory-based economy. Attempts were made to reconstruct the glories of medieval existence, and authenticity became the keyword.

Perhaps this was seen nowhere more clearly than in the tragic life of Thomas Chatterton, who committed suicide in 1770 at the age of seventeen, having written a series of poems which he attempted to pass off as the work of a fifteenth-century monk called Thomas Rowley. Not only are these poems fine in themselves, but they are remarkable for his care in trying to achieve authenticity in style and language.

Chatterton's attempt to evoke a fifteenth-century atmosphere includes choosing medieval subjects, such as 'The Battle of Hastings' or 'The Tournament' and describing the clothes, customs and historical events of the time in language interlaced with deliberately obscure words. In 'Eclogue the Second', for example, he chooses the theme of the Crusades:

> *Richard of lion's heart to fight is gone,*
> *Upon the broad sea do the banners gleam;*
> *The amenusèd nations be aston*
> *To see so large a fleet, so fine, so breme.*[2]

And 'The Tournament' reminds us of the fifteenth-century *Morte d'Arthur* of Malory, with its echoes of the age of chivalry:

> *Now by Saint Mary, if on all the field*
> *Y-crased spears and helmets be besprent,*
> *If every knight did hold a piercèd shield,*
> *If all the field with champions blood be stent*
> *Yet to encounter him I be content.*[3]

Although the taste for Gothic horror lingered on—and was still popular when Mary Shelley's *Frankenstein* appeared in 1818, and even much later in 1847, when Charlotte Brontë's Gothic *Jane Eyre* appeared, with its gloomy mansion, horrific happenings in the night and such weird touches as the three ghastly pictures Jane paints with such enjoyment—the historical interest in medievalism reflected in Chatterton's poems is an equally important element in popular novels from the end of the eighteenth century, particularly in the works of Sir Walter Scott.

Scott took his interest in medievalism seriously. Like Chatterton, he endeavoured to reproduce the language, dress and manners of the historical period he was representing as faithfully as possible, without falling into the error of being merely obscure. In his dedicatory epistle to *Ivanhoe* he wrote of the dangers likely to befall a writer who indulged in a blind love of things medieval:

> *he would act very injudiciously if he were to select from the glossary the obsolete words which it contains, and employ those exclusively of all phrases and vocables retained in modern days. This was the error of the unfortunate Chatterton. In order to give his language the appearance of antiquity, he rejected every word that was modern, and produced a dialect entirely different from any that had ever been spoken in Great Britain . . .* [The author's] *language must not be exclusively obsolete and unintelligible, but he should admit, if possible, no word or turn of phraseology betraying an origin directly modern.*

Following his own advice, Scott creates a language designed to be authentically medieval in tone without being *'obsolete and unintelligible'*. So, in *The Talisman*, King Richard jokes with De Vaux:

> *methinks a coif would become thy lowering features as well as a child's biggin would beseem mine.*

But it is not only in language that Scott aims for historical accuracy. His castles are carefully medieval, without the trappings of ruined chapels and subterranean passages that characterize the novels of Walpole or Mrs Radcliffe. In *Quentin Durward* the order goes out:

> *Up with every drawbridge, and down with every portcullis— let the gates of the town be trebly guarded . . . Draw the floating bridge to the right-hand side of the river.*

Costumes, too, are described with care; Durward's uncle, the Archer, wears:

*gorget, arm-pieces, and gauntlets . . . of the finest steel,
curiously inlaid with silver, and his hauberk, or shirt of mail,
was as clear and bright as the frost-work of a winter morning
. . . his knees and legs were protected by a hose of mail and shoes
of steel . . . a broad strong poniard hung by his right side . . .
the baldric for his two-handed sword, richly embroidered,
hung upon his left shoulder.*

But while Chatterton and Scott gave the public a good imitation
of medieval life and literature, a new vogue arose for the real thing.
The works of Dante, Petrarch, Boccaccio, Tasso, Chaucer and
Spenser were 'rediscovered', and new editions enabled their works
to reach a wider, and highly appreciative audience. In his series of
lectures, *On the English Poets*, given in 1818, Hazlitt refers to the
*'four greatest names in English poetry, . . . Chaucer, Spenser, Shake-
speare and Milton'*, and regrets that little attention has previously
been paid to Chaucer and Spenser, who *'either never emerged far
above the horizon, or were too soon involved in the obscurity of time'*.
He also points out that *'Chaucer . . . became thoroughly imbued with
the spirit and excellences of the great Italian poets and prosewriters,
Dante, Petrarch and Boccace.'* Here Hazlitt is directing his audience's
mind back past the sham medievalism popular at the time, and
encouraging them to discover the qualities of the originals for themselves. It was a discovery which had already been made with delight
by both Keats and Shelley.

The early poems of Keats are full of references to Petrarch,
Spenser, and Tasso. Indeed, what was probably his first poem,
written in 1812, is 'Imitation of Spenser'. His 'Ode to Apollo' of
1815 mentions Spenser and Tasso among the great bards, while in
1816 his 'Epistle to Charles Cowden Clarke' shows his interest in
The Faerie Queene:

> *And lovely Una in a leafy nook,
> And Archimago leaning o'er his book.*[4]

Later poems refer to *'lovely Laura'* and her *'faithful Petrarch'* or
'eloquent and famed Boccaccio', and 'Isabella, or the Pot of Basil' is
a rewriting of the fifth novel of the fourth day from Boccaccio's
Decameron.

And yet Keats' interest in things medieval is by no means a dry,
academic one. Indeed, it is the direct, forcible appeal to his imagination in the Gothic horror novels or in the pseudo-medieval poems
of Chatterton which comes across most strongly in his poetry. In

'The Eve of St Mark', Keats even follows Chatterton in writing mock-medieval verse:

> *Als writith he of swevenis,*
> *Men han beforne they wake in bliss,*
> *Whanne that hir friendes thinke hem bound*
> *In crimped shroude farre under grounde.*[5]

In 'Isabella', too, Keats adds a touch of his own to Boccaccio's story, giving a Gothic thrill of horror in the description of Lorenzo's head — *'The thing was vile with green and livid spot'*.

The appeal of Gothic to Keats was not simply a morbid taste for horror; rather, it fulfilled his keenly-felt belief that all aspects of life were, if seen aright, beautiful, even that which at first sight appeared repellent. To the poet, every kind of experience was valid material. In his letter to Woodhouse, dated 27 October, 1818, Keats expounds this idea at some length:

> *As to the poetical Character itself . . . it is everything and nothing—it has no character—it enjoys light and shade; it lives in gusto, be it foul or fair, high or low, rich or poor, mean or elevated—it has as much delight in conceiving an Iago as an Imogen. What shocks the virtuous philosopher, delights the camelion Poet.*[6]

He had earlier given full proof of his delight in things *'foul'* as well as *'fair'*, when he described, in his letter of early July to Thomas Keats, the old crone he calls *'The Duchess of Dunghill'*.

> *a squalid old woman squat like an ape . . . with a pipe in her mouth and looking out with a round-eyed skinny lidded inanity . . . squab and lean she sat and puff'd out the smoke . . . What a thing would be a history of her life and sensations.*[7]

Keats was himself conscious of an element of Gothic horror in the popular tradition in his poetry. Writing to his brother George in a letter dated February, 1819, he promises to send copies of:

> *the 'Pot of Basil', 'St Agnes eve', and if I should have finished it a little thing called the 'eve of St Mark.'*

He adds,

> *you see what fine mother Radcliff names I have.*[8]

The poem which is most consciously 'medieval' in setting and language is 'The Eve of St Agnes'. The story owes much to *Romeo and Juliet*, itself taken from a tale by the sixteenth-century Italian writer, Bandello. Characters such as the beadsman and Angela are obvious counterparts to Friar Lawrence and Juliet's nurse. There are numerous touches which suggest a medieval castle and its inhabitants—'The sculptur'd dead . . . knights, ladies'; 'many a sweeping train'; 'buttress'd from moonlight'; 'hot-blooded lords'; 'lowly arched way'; 'dusky gallery'; 'casement high and triple-arch'd'; 'hollow lute'; 'chain-droop'd lamp'; 'the arras'; 'the footworn stones'. But Keats is not content with mere description; he endeavours to create a feeling of authenticity through his actual choice of words, so that Angela, for example, urging Porphyro to 'hie thee from this place', adds:

> Thou must hold water in a witch's sieve,
> And be liege-lord of all the Elves and Fays
> To venture so,[9]

and when she agrees to help him, goes to fetch 'cates and dainties'.

Keats' poems, then, indicate an interest which embraces both a delight in original fourteenth-, fifteenth- and sixteenth-century literature, and the late eighteenth-century fashion for Gothic. Exactly the same broad-based interest is evident in the works of Shelley.

On the one hand, we have Shelley describing in a letter of July, 1818, how 'We have almost finished Ariosto' and adding:

> How different from the tender and solemn enthusiasm of Petrarch—or even the delicate moral sensibility of Tasso.[10]

In April of the same year he had described Milan Cathedral, 'with its stained glass and massy granite columns' and added:

> There is one solitary spot among these aisles, behind the altar, where the light of day is dim and yellow under the storied window, which I have chosen to visit, and read Dante there.[11]

Yet if, like Keats, Shelley was genuinely interested in medieval literature, he also felt the appeal of a 'Mother Radcliffe' sort of story. In her Preface to Frankenstein, Mary Shelley tells us how she and Shelley spent 'a wet, ungenial summer' reading 'volumes of ghost stories'. She describes some which are, in the real Gothic tradition, full of hauntings and gloomy castles, adding:

> I have not seen these stories since then, but their incidents are as fresh in my mind as if I had read them yesterday.

Shelley's natural interest in and enjoyment of horror stories meant that he was instantly fascinated when he heard of the gruesome story of the Cenci family. It was a fascination shared by the

Italian public; in his Preface to *The Cenci*, the play he wrote on the subject, he tells us that:

> *On my arrival at Rome I found that the story of the Cenci was a subject not to be mentioned in Italian society without awakening a deep and breathless interest.*

From his comments on his confidence in the appeal it would have for an English audience, it seems likely that he was hoping to exploit the current fashion for Gothic horror, and write something which, for once, would be sure to appeal to the general public. He was at pains to point out that it was definitely to the popular taste:

> *It is written without any of the peculiar feelings and opinions which characterize my other compositions . . . there is nothing beyond what the multitude are contented to believe that they can understand, either in imagery, opinion, or sentiment.*

Certainly, Mrs Radcliffe or 'Monk' Lewis might have invented the story of the Cenci, so terror-laden is their history. And Shelley's treatment of it is wholly in the Gothic tradition. The tone is set in the Preface, where he describes the Cenci Palace in true 'Mother Radcliffe' terms:

> *The Cenci Palace is . . . a vast and gloomy pile of feudal architecture . . . and from the upper windows you see the immense ruins of Mount Palatine half hidden under their profuse overgrowth of trees . . . One of the gates of the Palace formed of immense stones and leading through a passage, dark and lofty and opening into gloomy subterranean chambers, struck me particularly.*

The plot itself contains all the elements of the Gothic grotesque: Count Francesco Cenci is a tyrant, delighting in the torment of his wife Lucretia and of his children, to whom Lucretia is stepmother. He exults in the death of two of his sons, announcing their demise at a triumphal banquet. He deliberately ruins the marriage of his son Giacomo, by poisoning the minds of the latter's wife and children with lies. We learn that he has imposed strange cruelties on his children:

> *And he has given us all*
> *Ditch-water, and the fever-stricken flesh*
> *Of buffaloes, and bade us eat or starve,*
> *And we have eaten—He has made me look*

> *On my beloved Bernardo, when the rust*
> *Of heavy chains has gangrened his sweet limbs.*[12]

Finally he rapes his own daughter, Beatrice—though this is never explicitly stated, merely indicated by dark hints—and she plots his murder. Torture and ignominious death follow for Beatrice, Lucretia and Giacomo, but the final note of the play is one of triumph for Beatrice, who finds a calm dignity in death after her life of exquisite misery.

It is perhaps worth noting that Shelley had felt his talents were unsuited to writing a play. And yet in this his only true drama (for *Prometheus*, 'Swellfoot the Tyrant' and *Hellas* have no pretensions to the stage) he shows a sure touch as a playwright. The work opens with a line immediately calculated to jolt the audience into attention:

> *That matter of the murder is hushed up,*

and the following two lines are no less startling, for they at once suggest one of Shelley's favourite themes—the corruption of the Church—and place the word *'Holiness'* in bitter proximity to the word *'murder'*.

Throughout the play, Shelley skilfully balances suspense against terror and pity, as we wait to see what news of his sons the Count will reveal at his banquet; or whether the murder attempt on the way to Petrella has succeeded; or whether the hired assassins will carry out the deed; or whether Beatrice will be released by the law.

Yet Shelley's own dramatic skills owe more than a little to Shakespeare, who was seen as a 'medieval' writer and was greatly admired by the Romantics as exhibiting the stirring imaginative qualities denied by eighteenth-century Classical restraint. *The Cenci* contains obvious echoes of *King Lear*—for example, the curse which Count Cenci puts on Beatrice in Act IV, scene one, is strongly reminiscent of Lear's curses on Goneril—and of *Measure for Measure*, where Claudio's

> *Ay, but to die, and go we know not where;*
> *To lie in cold obstruction, and to rot*

becomes in Shelley:

> *Can it be possible I have*
> *To die so suddenly? So young to go*
> *Under the obscure, cold, rotting, wormy ground!*
> *To be nailed down into a narrow place.*[13]

But it is to *Macbeth* that Shelley owes the greatest debt. Echoes of it abound, from the ghoulish feast where Beatrice warns that:

> *with avenging looks*
> *My brothers' ghosts should hunt thee from thy seat*[14]

—a clear reminder of Banquo—to Giacomo listening to the bell, like Lady Macbeth, *'One! Two!'* Nor can we fail to notice Shelley's *'Would that it were done'*, like Macbeth's *'If 'twere done, when 'tis done. . . .'*, and Shelley's borrowed use of *'multitudinous'* after a comment on sleep and conscience.

The scene where Count Cenci is murdered is lifted almost wholesale from *Macbeth*. Shakespeare's:

> *'Did not you speak?'*
> *'When?'*
> *'Now.'*
> *'As I descended.'*

becomes in Shelley:

> *'Did not you call?'*
> *'When?'*
> *'Now.'*
> *'I ask if all is over.'*[15]

Lady Macbeth's comment,

> *Had he not resembled*
> *My father as he slept, I had done it,*

changes to Shelley's:

> *We dare not kill an old and sleeping man; . . .*
> *I knew it was the ghost*
> *Of my dead father speaking through his lips*
> *And could not kill him.*[16]

And, just as in *Macbeth*, the murder of the Count is followed by the unexpected arrival at the castle of a deputation to see the murdered man.

But Shelley does not merely borrow lines from Shakespeare; more importantly, he captures the passion, the terror, the pity and the vitality which made Shakespeare such an admired model for the Romantic writers striving to escape the narrow bounds of the Classical ideal.

The taste for medievalism was part of that escape. Looking back on the fashions for Gothic castles, tales of horror, and novels full of fantasy and the supernatural, critics have often puzzled over it, as

19. *Lady Macbeth Seizing the Daggers* by H. Fuseli. The Romantic delight in horror and wild imaginings is here linked by Fuseli to the great interest in Shakespeare at this period. (Tate Gallery, London)

a strange aberration, and seemed to ask, with Jane Austen, *'What ideas have you been admitting?'* Part of the answer, perhaps, is that the appeal of medievalism lay not merely in its obscurity, not simply in the grotesque, not only in the exotic strangeness of it all in its complete contrast to Augustan formality, but also in the vital and vivid stimulus it gave to the imagination of both poets and public.

[1] S. T. Coleridge (ed. by Shawcross) *Biographia Literaria* (vol. 2) (O.U.P., 1939) pp. 183–4   [2] Thomas Chatterton 'Eclogue the Second' 3–6   [3] Thomas Chatterton 'Tournament' 131–35   [4] 'To Charles Cowden Clarke' 36–7   [5] 'The Eve of St Mark' 99–102   [6] K.L. pp. 221–2   [7] *ibid*. p. 173   [8] *ibid*. p. 264   [9] 'The Eve of St Agnes' XIV (3–5)   [10] P. B. Shelley (ed. by R. B. Johnson) *Letters of Shelley* (Bodley Head, 1929) p. 93   [11] *ibid*. p. 90   [12] *The Cenci* Act II, scene I, 66–71   [13] *ibid*. Act V, scene IV, 48–51   [14] *ibid*. Act I, scene III, 152–3   [15] *ibid*. Act IV, scene III, 8   [16] *ibid*. Act IV, scene III, 9; 20–2

8

The Changing Face of Nature

Even the most cursory reading of Shakespeare's *King Lear*, written in the early seventeenth century, reveals at once that the words 'nature' and 'natural' are being used in several senses. Lear's follower is a *'natural'*—a fool. Gloucester has a *'natural'*—that is, illegitimate—son in Edmund, whom he thinks is more *'natural'*—naturally affectionate—than his legitimate son Edgar. Similarly, a reading of early eighteenth- and early nineteenth-century texts reveals a continuous intense interest in 'nature', but a great diversity in the meaning of the term between these two periods.

In the first half of the eighteenth century, we find that the term is frequently used to refer to a carefully ordered cosmic plan. 'Nature' is seen as highly organized; there is no sense of wildness, no hint of an uncontrolled state. Indeed, Pope, writing 'An Essay on Man' in 1730–2, far from contrasting nature with art, as earlier writers had often done, asserts that:

> *All Nature is but Art, unknown to thee;*
> *All Chance, Direction, which thou canst not see;*
> *All Discord, Harmony, not understood;*
> *All partial Evil, universal Good.*[1]

The *'Art'* which was displayed in *'Nature'* was basically the great 'Chain of Being'; this refers to the idea that there is a progression of creation from God above, down through angels, men, animals and plants to nothingness. Every creature has his allotted place on this chain, so that nature involves a high degree of organization:

> *Vast chain of being, which from God began,*
> *Natures ethereal, human, angel, man,*
> *Beast, bird, fish, insect! what no eye can see,*
> *No glass can reach! from Infinite to thee,*
> *From thee to Nothing! . . .*
> *Where, one step broken, the great scale's destroyed;*
> *From Nature's chain whatever link you strike,*
> *Tenth or ten thousandth, breaks the chain alike.*[2]

This view of nature as carefully controlled was embodied in the gardens of the period. In the late seventeenth century there had been little attempt at naturalness in gardening; on the contrary, the carefully patterned layout popularized by Le Nôtre's work on the grounds of the palace of Versailles had led to great stress on formality and balance. By Pope's time, however, we see in the gardens the same feeling for 'ordered naturalness' that is evident in 'Essay on Man'.

Landscape gardening became the fashion, and practitioners such as the famous 'Capability' Brown removed the formal, straight-lined patterns outlined by box-hedges, and replaced them with vistas of lakes and woodland, equally planned and ordered, but now along rococo curves.

Eighteenth-century landscaping, such as that associated with Brown, is charmingly described by Jane Austen—herself a very eighteenth-century figure in many of her tastes—in *Pride and Prejudice* when Elizabeth Bennet visits Mr Darcy's seat of Pemberley:

> *Pemberley House . . . was a large, handsome stone building, standing well on rising ground, and backed by a ridge of high woody hills;—and in front, a stream of some natural importance was swelled into greater, but without any artificial appearance. Its banks were neither formal, nor falsely adorned. Elizabeth . . . had never seen a place for which nature had done more, or where natural beauty had been so little counteracted by an awkward taste.*

A real-life Pemberley is Blenheim Palace in Oxfordshire, a mansion begun as a mark of gratitude to the Duke of Marlborough for his victories over the French in the reign of Queen Anne. The original plan for the grounds was a formal layout, but later Capability Brown was called in to make the view more 'natural'—which he achieved by the identical practice described at Pemberley: damming a river to make a lake, *'but without any artificial appearance'*.

Later in the eighteenth century, tastes were even more strongly for the natural look, and a fashion developed for the 'picturesque', the essence of which was a quality of surprise. The surprise, however, was of a carefully controlled variety, and included well-cared-for 'wildernesses' as Jane Austen describes at Sotherton in *Mansfield Park*, where:

> *A considerable flight of steps landed them in the wilderness, which was a planted wood of about two acres, and though*

*chiefly of larch and laurel, and beech cut down, and though laid
out with too much regularity, was darkness and shade, and
natural beauty, compared with the bowling-green and the
terrace.*

But if Nature in the first half of the eighteenth century went
hand in hand with control, order, custom, formality, and the kind
of civilized neatness of the countryside Cobbett later described near
Guildford:

*The road is good; the soil is good; the houses are neat; the
people are neat; the hills, the woods, the meadows, all are
beautiful. Nothing wild and bold, to be sure: but exceedingly
pretty,*

in the second half of the century the influence of Rousseau was at
work, urging in many of his writings, such as *La Nouvelle Héloise,
Emile* and *A Discourse on the Origin of Inequality*, the idea of a return
to nature, an abandonment of formal society, and the happiness
achieved by renouncing the customs of mankind.

This was not entirely a new idea. In the sixteenth and seventeenth
centuries, the vision of the 'noble savage' had been much discussed,
and the view of travellers praising apparently paradisaical primitive
societies was set against the view of voyagers attacked by hostile
savages. The debate, for example, engaged Shakespeare in *The
Tempest*, where we have to consider whether the wild Caliban is any
more savage than the supposedly civilized Antonio, or whether
Miranda, brought up on the island, is anything less than perfectly
civilized. A late seventeenth-century view of the 'noble savage' may
be found in Mrs Behn's novel, *Oroonoko*, where the native prince is
a composite of every grace and all nobility:

*'twas amazing to imagine where it was he learn'd so much
humanity or, to give his accomplishments a juster name, where
'twas he got that real greatness of soul, those refined notions
of true honour, that absolute generosity, and that softness that
was capable of the highest passions of love and gallantry . . .
the most illustrious courts could not have produced a braver
man, both for greatness of courage and mind, a judgement
more solid, a wit more quick, and a conversation more sweet
and diverting.*

A similar viewpoint also appears nearly fifty years later in the
work we have already noted for its orderly view of nature—Pope's

'An Essay on Man'. Since, in the natural world, all is planned and *'whatever is, is right,'* Pope sees primitive man as noble and virtuous:

> *Nor think, in NATURE'S STATE they blindly trod;*
> *The state of Nature was the reign of God:*
> *Self-love and Social at her birth began,*
> *Union the bond of all things, and of Man . . .*
> *Heaven's attribute was Universal Care,*
> *And Man's prerogative to rule, but spare.*[3]

The difference between Pope's view and Rousseau's is that Pope sees natural man as happy *in society*, albeit a primitive one, whereas for Rousseau an abandonment of society is essential for virtue. In *A Discourse on the Origin of Inequality*, he describes the happy state of savages who are completely independent. While they were contented with the bare necessities of life:

> *so long as they undertook only what a single person could accomplish, and confined themselves to such arts as did not require the joint labour of several hands, they lived free, healthy, honest and happy lives . . . But from the moment one man began to stand in need of the help of another; from the moment it appeared advantageous to any one man to have enough provisions for two, equality disappeared, property was introduced, work became indispensable and . . . slavery and misery were soon seen to germinate and grow up with the crops.*

It is difficult to say how, and in what precise order, fashions change and ideas alter. But it is clear that Rousseau revived the idea of the 'noble savage', and that, in combination with his influential political writings, these ideas led people to look away from the customs of society and the formality of their usual surroundings, and to take a fresh look at nature as a source of inspiration. At the same time, as we have seen, tastes in gardening were moving towards the 'picturesque' with its element of wildness and surprise, while in architecture the exotic, both Eastern and Gothic, was growing popular, and, as described in Chapter 7, specially built Gothic ruins were a familiar sight. In the field of literature, the taste for the horrifying and amazing in novels went alongside a growing desire for 'naturalness' in poetry.

In all these ways, the late eighteenth century began to express its Romanticism, and in particular its growing dissatisfaction with the order, control, and tightness of the Age of Reason, and with the materialism and bleakness of the Industrial Age. But the new-found

love of nature was very much more than a simple enjoyment of the
natural world, and a feeling that the countryside was more peaceful
than the town. Many eighteenth-century writers had expressed in
pastoral poetry their dissatisfaction with urban existence. Dr Johnson's satirical poem 'On London' contrasts the city where

> *Malice, Rapine, Accident, conspire*
> *And now a Rabble rages, now a fire;*

with the countryside where

> *ev'ry Bush with Nature's Music rings,*
> *. . . ev'ry Breeze bears Health upon its Wings,*

and the joys of the countryside were vividly depicted—and often,
in spite of a widespread modern belief to the contrary, depicted with
a keen eye for detail—by poets such as Thomson, whose work 'The
Seasons' shows a real delight in nature. Indeed, though his language
is more formal, his 'Winter' obviously did much to inspire the opening of 'The Eve of St Agnes':

> *The Hare*
> *Tho' timorous of Heart, and hard beset*
> *By Death in various Forms, dark snares and Dogs,*
> *And more unpitying Man, the Garden seeks,*
> *Urg'd on by fearless Want. The bleating kind*
> *Eye the black Heaven, and next the glistening Earth,*
> *With Looks of dumb despair.*

To the Romantic poets, to Wordsworth at the end of the eighteenth
century, as to Keats and Shelley, twenty years later, the natural
world was not simply pretty; nor was it attractive because it offered
an *escape* from reality. On the contrary, its importance lay in its
ability to offer a completely new set of spiritual values.

The first move towards this view of nature came with the
realization that order, neatness and control, in nature as in man,
do not necessarily make for greatness and nobility. The German
poet Goethe—in his novel *Sorrows of Young Werther*, published in
1774, and extremely influential in England—expresses this theme
through the mouth of the young painter:

> *Nature alone is infinitely rich, and Nature alone forms the*
> *great artist. Much can be adduced in favour of rules . . .*
> *The man who models himself on them will never produce any-*
> *thing inferior or in bad taste . . . but there will be an end to*
> *. . . his art.*

Keats was later to express precisely the same views when he wrote to his publisher that *'if Poetry comes not as naturally as the Leaves to a tree it had better not come at all'*.

An early manifestation of the growing taste for wildness and the obviously uncontrolled was the new fashion for mountain scenery. It may seem surprising today, when mountaineering is a popular pastime and Alpine views have become a cliché, that, until the late eighteenth century, mountains were generally considered simply a nuisance. Writing in *History Today*, Professor Ronald Rees describes how:

> *seventeenth-century English writers and poets . . . referred to mountains in the most disapproving terms. James Howell objected to the 'monstrous abruptness' of the Pyrenees and found the Alps 'high and hideous', dismissing them as 'monstrous excrescences of Nature' . . . Sentiments such as these persisted into the eighteenth and even into the nineteenth centuries. In 1738 Dr Johnson referred to the 'hopeless sterility of the Scottish Hills' which had been 'dismissed by nature from her care.'*

And yet only a year later the poet Gray wrote to his mother from Turin, where he was travelling with Horace Walpole, describing the experience of crossing the Alps in glowing terms:

> *The immensity of the precipices, the soaring of the river and torrents that run into it, the huge crags covered with ice and snow, and the clouds below you and about you are objects it is impossible to conceive without seeing them.*[4]

To his friend Richard West, he was even more expansive:

> *I do not remember to have gone ten paces without an exclamation, that there was no restraining: Not a precipice, not a torrent, not a cliff, but is pregnant with religion and poetry.*[5]

As this idea that mountains embodied all the most wonderful qualities of nature grew more popular, they became part of the taste for 'the sublime'. This was a term applied to anything beyond control and comprehension which yet aroused feelings of wonder and awe. A good description of what the eighteenth-century writer meant by the sublime can be found in the essay 'On the Sublime and Beautiful' by the statesman Edmund Burke, published in 1756. He describes how 'the sublime' must arouse deep feelings, more of terror than delight:

> *Whatever is fitted in any sort to excite the ideas of pain and*
> *danger, that is to say, whatever is in any sort terrible, or is*
> *conversant about terrible objects, is a source of the sublime;*
> *that is, it is productive of the strongest emotion which the mind*
> *is capable of feeling.*

Such ideas were strengthened and popularized by the mountainous scenery included in best-selling works of fiction, such as Mrs
Radcliffe's *The Mysteries of Udolpho*, published in 1794, where the
Alps are not only described, but specifically shown to arouse intense
feelings:

> *From Beaujeu the road had constantly ascended, conducting*
> *the travellers into the higher regions of the air, where immense*
> *glaciers exhibited their frozen horrors, and eternal snow*
> *whitened the summits of the mountains. They often paused to*
> *contemplate these stupendous scenes, and, seated on some wild*
> *cliff, where only the ilex or the larch could flourish, looked over*
> *the dark forests of fir, and precipices where human foot had*
> *never wandered, into the glen . . . The serenity and clearness of*
> *the air in these high regions were particularly delightful to the*
> *travellers; it seemed to inspire them with a finer spirit, and*
> *diffused an indescribable complacency* over their minds. They*
> *had no words to express the sublime emotions they felt.*

It is noteworthy that the mountains are not simply regarded as
beautiful or breathtaking; their role is more positive and moral,
for they arouse *'a finer spirit'*. And this is typical of the late eighteenth-
century feeling for mountains which were seen as able to inspire the
purity and realization of a better life such as Rousseau had felt could
be found in a return to nature. Indeed, they themselves symbolized
a return to nature, for mountains such as the Alps, or, nearer home,
the Scottish Highlands, were inevitably the home of isolated com-
munities unspoilt by much contact with a sophisticated, materialistic society. Both aspects of mountain life—the moral inspiration,
and the return to simplicity—can be seen in the poetry of William
Wordsworth, which emerged upon the English literary scene at the
end of the eighteenth century, and which was both a result and a
cause of a popular desire to 'return to nature'.

Wordsworth was one of the 'Lake' school of poets, that is, a group
of three poets (himself, Coleridge and Southey) who lived in the
English Lake District. Wordsworth, in particular, advocated a return

* i.e. a tranquil pleasure.

to simple language and homely events in poetry. He decided to 'choose incidents and situations from common life' and many of the 'incidents' he described show the moral effects of nature—especially the hills and mountains of the north of England—upon himself and on simple country folk. In his autobiographical poem *The Prelude*, subtitled 'Growth of a Poet's mind', he describes how his love of nature and, at the same time, his fear of its awesomeness—its sublimity—moulded and formed him. His was, after a fashion, an *Emile* type of education where the child learns by experience and by the impressions borne in upon him from the natural world, whether these impressions be peaceful or disturbing:

Dust as we are, the immortal Spirit grows
Like harmony in music; there is a dark
Inscrutable workmanship that reconciles
Discordant elements, makes them cling together
In one society. How strange that all
The terrors, pains and early miseries,
Regrets, vexations, lassitudes interfused
Within my mind, should e'er have borne a part,
And that a needful part, in making up
The calm existence that is mine when I
Am worthy of myself! Praise to the end!
Thanks to the means which Nature deigned to employ;
Whether her fearless visitings, or those
That came with soft alarm, like hurtless light
Opening the peaceful clouds; or she may use
Severer interventions, ministry
More palpable, as best might suit her aim.[6]

Inspired partly by the growing taste for Wordsworth's poetry, after initial harsh critical reaction, and partly by the continuing interest in the exotic and the wild, tourists flocked to the Lake District, which suddenly became an amazingly popular tourist resort. Simultaneously, the fashionable liking for mountains was being reflected in the work of artists such as Richard Wilson, whose painting *Cader Idris* depicts the angular sharpness of his native Welsh scenery. Early pictures by Turner, such as *Buttermere Lake*, and such paintings as *Valley of Zion* by John Cozens, all celebrated the growing interest in the inspirational quality of mountainous scenery—an interest which received a new impetus from the novels of Walter Scott. As Scott's popularity grew—and it grew at an incredible rate, so that his novels were sold by the thousands on the

20. *Llyn-y-Cau, Cader Idris* by R. Wilson. Mountains, which had always seemed merely an inconvenience to travellers, became more and more popular as the eighteenth century progressed. (Tate Gallery, London)

day of publication—the mountains of Scotland became familiar in imagination to countless men and women who never had, and never would, actually see them. In Scott, as in Mrs Radcliffe and Wordsworth, mountains are not merely breathtaking to look at, though they are certainly that; they ennoble the feelings and inspire the soul. A passage from *Rob Roy* illustrates this:

> *A sharp frost-wind, which made itself heard and felt from time to time, removed the clouds of mist which might otherwise have slumbered till morning on the valley; and though it could not totally disperse the clouds of vapour, yet threw them in confused and changeful masses, now hovering round the heads of the mountains, now filling, as with a dense and voluminous stream of smoke, the various deep gullies where masses of the composite rock, or brescia, tumbling in fragments from the cliffs, have rushed to the valley, leaving each behind its course a rent and torn ravine . . . The moon . . . silvered the windings of the river and the peaks and precipices which the mist left visible while her beams seemed as it were absorbed by the fleecy whiteness of the mist . . . Despite the uncertainty of my situation, a view so romantic, joined to the active and inspiring influence of the frosty atmosphere, elevated my spirits while it braced my nerves.*

21. *Buttermere Lake with Part of Cromackwater, Cumberland, a Shower* by J. M. W. Turner. The Lake District became a popular area for tourists as the fashion for 'wild' scenery grew. (Tate Gallery, London)

Exactly the same idea is apparent in a work of a very different nature from *Rob Roy*—Mary Shelley's *Frankenstein*, published in 1818, a year after Scott's tale of the wild outlaw achieved such popularity. Frankenstein, the scientist, stricken with grief at the outcome of his creation of a monster, roams the Alps in an attempt to calm his mind. He describes the *'abrupt sides of vast mountains'* where the only sounds are those of the avalanche or cracking ice. Far from being made gloomier by his surroundings,

> *These sublime and magnificent scenes afforded me the greatest consolation that I was capable of receiving. They elevated me from all littleness of feeling, and although they did not remove my grief, they subdued and tranquilised it.*

By the time Keats and Shelley were writing, then, the view of Nature as a well-ordered machine in which man was a necessary cog had given place to a view of Nature as the great inspirer, the purifier of souls, the healer of men as opposed to the corrupt influence of society. Nature, one might say, was now on the side of the revolutionary elements in the state, and it was no accident that the months of the new French Revolutionary Calendar were named, not after great leaders, but after the seasons and types of weather.

When John Keats set off with Charles Brown on a walking tour of the Lake District and the Scottish Highlands in the summer of 1818, he was following the general trend; he was not going for the exercise, nor just to see beautiful views, but to be improved morally, elevated emotionally, and inspired poetically:

> *I should not have consented to myself these four Months tramping in the highlands but that I thought it would give me more experience, rub off more Prejudice, use (me) to more hardship, identify finer scenes, load me with grander Mountains, and strengthen more my reach in Poetry, than would stopping at home among Books even though I should reach Homer.*[7]

He found some inspiration, certainly, but he also found a great deal of discomfort and made the discovery that one can have too much of a good thing. Writing to his friend Benjamin Bailey in July, 1818, he complains:

> *I have been among wilds and Mountains too much to break out much about the(i)r Grandeur.*[8]

This feeling seems to have stayed with him, for certainly mountains do not figure largely in his poetry, unlike that of Shelley—though admittedly Shelley had seen the Alps. For Shelley mountains were extremely important symbolically, and do represent a real source of inspiration and regeneration. This can be seen in *Prometheus Unbound*, for though Prometheus is

> *Nailed to this wall of eagle-baffling mountain,*
> *Black, wintry, dead, unmeasured; without herb*
> *Insect, or beast, or shape or sound of life,*[9]

his suffering on the mountain seems to endue him with the qualities of the mountain, its strength and power—what Mary Shelley in her notes on the poem calls *'fortitude and hope and the spirit of triumph'*. Similarly, it is on a mountain-top that Laon and Cythna in 'The Revolt of Islam' fulfil their love and achieve the sense of calm fortitude which enables them to face the tyrant:

> *Through the desert night we sped, while she alway*
> *Gazed on a mountain which we neared, whose crest*
> *Crowned with a marble ruin, in the ray*
> *Of the obscure stars gleamed . . . now*
> *A power, a thirst, a knowledge, which below*

All thoughts, like light beyond the atmosphere
Clothing its clouds with grace doth ever flow
Came on us, as we sate in silence there,
Beneath the golden stars of the clear azure air.[10]

Keats and Shelley may depict different aspects of nature, but they share a common purpose in attempting to show, as Wordsworth had, the unity of all creation. For Wordsworth, it is a mystical unity, when his very soul leaves his body and he becomes at one with nature:

even the motion of our human blood
Almost suspended, we are laid asleep
In body, and become a living soul:
While with an eye made quiet by the power
Of harmony, and the deep power of joy,
We see into the life of things.[11]

For Shelley, most important is the Platonic sense of an ideal universe —a millennium, a new Hellas—where perfect man will be at one with essential nature, for:

All things by a law divine
In one spirit meet and mingle.[12]

And to Keats, there is the belief, repeated over and over in letters and poetry, that there is an essential harmony between all things, and that the poet must continually partake of the existence of all other creatures—

The Sun, the Moon, the Sea and Men and Women.[13]

But man's relationship with Nature is twofold; he is to be at one with her ultimately, but she herself is to be his teacher, and help him to attain that unity. As Wordsworth describes watching the flowers and being led to share their enjoyment, so that his heart *'dances with the daffodils'*, so Keats and Shelley both endeavour through a keen observation of nature to enter into the life of natural objects. In 'The Cloud', for example, Shelley *becomes* the cloud, singing in an insistent, rolling rhythm about the endless circular motion of his existence:

I am the daughter of Earth and Water
And the nursling of the sky
I pass through the pores of the ocean and shores;
I change, but I cannot die.

For after the rain when with never a stain
The pavilion of Heaven is bare,
And the winds and sunbeams with their convex gleams
Build up the blue dome of air,
I silently laugh at my own Cenotaph,
And out of the caverns of rain,
Like a child from the womb, like a ghost from the tomb,
I arise and unbuild it again.

Keats, too, expresses the same sense of harmony with nature when he writes that *'if a sparrow come before my Window I take part in its existence and pick about the Gravel'.* So, in 'Ode to a Nightingale', he not only desires to *'fade away into the forest dim'*, but, through *'the viewless wings of Poesy'*, he partakes of the nightingale's existence and is *'Already with thee . . .'* On a different level, his ability to enter into another's existence is shared with his readers, when the apparently objective description of Lamia's change from snake to woman becomes of such intensity that we feel the agony ourselves —perhaps particularly because Keats jars our senses from complacency by the unnatural association of *'scarlet'* with *'pain'*. And Keats makes us further aware of the sense in which all experiences of man enter into a mystical harmony with nature by instinctively using imagery drawn from the natural world, even when describing man-made objects, like Madeline's window

Innumerable of stains and splendid dyes
As are the tiger-moth's deep-damask'd wings,[14]

or a human emotion, like melancholy—

when the melancholy fit shall fall
Sudden from heaven like a weeping cloud
That fosters the droop-headed flowers all
And hides the green hill in an April shroud.[15]

Man at one with nature, then, is the desire of the Romantics. But it is not a sentimental rusticity which they desire, not the kind of temporary escape from sophistication which made eighteenth-century court ladies play at being milkmaids for an afternoon or which led to the Augustan vogue for pastoral poetry. For Keats and Shelley and their contemporaries, a return to the pure and unmaterialistic emotions associated with rural as opposed to urban life, and wild as opposed to cultivated scenery, was an essential precursor of the new kind of society which they felt to be so eminently desirable.

[1] Alexander Pope 'An Essay on Man' Epistle I, 289–92   [2] *ibid.* Epistle I, 237–41; 244–46   [3] *ibid.* Epistle III, 147–50; 159–60   [4] Thomas Gray *Selected Letters of Thomas Gray* (O.U.P., 1951) p. 43   [5] *ibid.* p. 45   [6] William Wordsworth *The Prelude* Book I, 340–56   [7] K.L. p. 195   [8] *ibid.* pp. 195–6   [9] *Prometheus Unbound* Act 1, 20–22   [10] 'The Revolt of Islam' Canto VI, XXII (5–8); XXX (4–9)   [11] William Wordsworth 'Lines Composed a Few Miles above Tintern Abbey' 44–9   [12] P. B. Shelley 'Love's Philosophy' 6–7   [13] K.L. p. 222   [14] 'The Eve of St Agnes' XXIV (5–6)   [15] 'Ode on Melancholy' 11–14

9

The Changing Language

The eighteenth century, with its characteristics of self-discipline, restraint and control, was strongly influenced by classical antiquity. Roman, and later, Greek civilization, was admired as the type of perfection in all areas of human life, and especially in art, architecture and literature. A classical education was still considered essential for a well brought up young man, and written English relied heavily on latinate words—so much so that when Dr Johnson published his famous *Dictionary* in 1755, he felt it perfectly acceptable to define and explain terms in latinate phrases. A simple cough, for example, was described as: *'A convulsion of the lungs, vellicated by some sharp serosity'*.

Similarly, Pope's notes to his poem 'The Dunciad' (fully published in 1743) included many Latin quotations as part of their explanation. Much poetry was written *'in imitation of Pindar'* or *'in imitation of Juvenal'*. Even when reading lighter literature, the public was expected to have a knowledge of classical forms; for example, much of the humour of Fielding's novel *Tom Jones* (published 1749) would be lost on the reader who knew nothing of the heroic epic.

Much of this stress on the classics was the result of the belief that the ancients had discovered the 'rules' of good writing. A distinction was therefore drawn between the common, everyday use of language, and the more elevated style to be deliberately sought after and fostered in written works. It was particularly felt that the kind of vocabulary which might be suitable for prose would not be fitting for poetry.

'A poet should take particular care to guard himself against idiomatic ways of speaking,' wrote Addison in *The Spectator* in 1712, while, in 1739, Lord Chesterfield felt that the subject was of sufficient importance to warrant instructing his seven-year-old son on the matter:

> *Poetical diction, that is, poetical language, is more sublime and lofty than prose, and takes liberties which are not allowed in*

prose, and are called Poetical Licences. This difference between verse and prose you will easily observe, if you read them both with attention. In verse, things are seldom said plainly and simply, as one would say them in prose; but they are described and embellished; as, for example, what you hear the watchman say often in three words, 'a cloudy morning', is said thus in verse, in the tragedy of 'Cato':

> *'The dawn is overcast, the morning lowers,*
> *And heavily in clouds brings on the day.'*

This is poetical diction, which would be improper in prose, though each word separately may be used in prose.[1]

By the mid-eighteenth century, the use of such a deliberately elevated style had not merely become customary; it was seen by Dr Johnson as an essential for fine writing, and a particularly pleasing development of modern times:

> *There was before the time of Dryden no poetical diction, no system of words at once refined from the grossness of domestic use, and free from the harshness of terms appropriated to particular arts. Words too familiar, or too remote, defeat the purpose of a poet.*[2]

So it was that English poetry developed a tendency to periphrase— that is, expressing an idea in a roundabout way, so avoiding a vulgar preciseness. A reading of eighteenth-century poetry will quickly reveal the presence of terms such as 'umbrageous dales' for 'shady valleys'; 'scaly brood' for 'fish'; 'transparent wave', 'crystal flood' or 'limpid streams' for 'water'; and 'pure Cerulean' for 'sky'.

When, at the end of the eighteenth and beginning of the nineteenth centuries, writers of the Romantic movement rebelled against classical restraint, it was against just such a *'system of words refined from the grossness of domestic use'* that they revolted. In France, where the drama had been particularly inhibited by strict precepts as to which words were suitable, the writer Stendhal pointed out the stupidity of rules which forbade the use of the word 'pistol' in plays about battles, or the ludicrousness of an author having to find a roundabout way of saying 'cooking pot'. It was in reaction against such petty restrictions that the French dramatist Victor Hugo introduced words such as 'broomstick' into his play, *Hernani*, in 1830, thus scandalizing the purists. The Romantic writers felt that all words—as all experiences—were appropriate, if the poet was to suggest the rich variety of life. It was this willingness to partake fully, and *not* refine away less pleasant aspects of existence, which Keats called *'gusto'* and said was the essence of the poetic character.

Great writers, the Romantics felt, could use lowly words to express sublime and deep emotions. This was one of the traits they so admired in Shakespeare (who had been denounced by adherents of the Classical school in France, for breaking all the 'rules') for he had the ability to use the most common articles to create the most telling images. So Macbeth talks of sleep that *'knits up the ravell'd sleeve of care'* and Hamlet warns Gertrude not to *'spread the compost on the weeds'* of her sin.

The Romantic writers also objected to the restraint on poetic form. Much eighteenth-century English verse had been written in end-stopped rhyming couplets—which had been even more compulsory in French drama of the period—where the deliberately imposed pause at the end of the line was seen by its opponents as preventing the use of natural speech rhythms. An attempt to produce a really conversational flow of language in poetry was felt by the Romantics to be as important as an unrestrained vocabulary.

Those who wished to free language from restriction were reacting against the eighteenth-century desire to control it. In France, the

22. *Dr Johnson in the Ante-room of Lord Chesterfield, Waiting for an Audience, 1748* by E. M. Ward. Dr Johnson approached Lord Chesterfield hoping he would stand as patron to the projected Dictionary, but was refused. (Tate Gallery, London)

Academy, established in 1635, had for over a century been formulating the rules for literary excellence. In England, Dr Johnson set about writing his *Dictionary* with the aim of giving order to his native tongue, which, he said, had been

> *suffered to spread, under the direction of chance, into wild exuberance; resigned to the tyranny of time and fashion; and exposed to the corruptions of ignorance and caprices of innovation.*[3]

When embarking on his task, he had discovered that English speech was *'copious without order, and energetick without rules'.*[4] He now felt that he had been over-optimistic, but his original aim was to

> *fix our language, and put a stop to those alterations which time and chance have hitherto suffered to make in it without opposition.*[5]

The Romantic rebels took an exactly opposite view. Their theory is summed up by Victor Hugo in his 'Preface to *Cromwell*' which was regarded as the manifesto of the French Romantics:

> *A language does not fix itself. The human spirit is always on the march . . . and languages with it . . . Every age has its own ideas, it must also have words suitable to these ideas. Languages are like the sea, they are perpetually oscillating.*

What might be termed the manifesto of the English Romantics, at least as far as the use of language was concerned, was Wordsworth's Preface to the second edition of *Lyrical Ballads* (1800). Wordsworth condemned the *'gaudiness and inane phraseology of many modern writers'*—what Hazlitt later summed up as *'tantalizing, teasing, tripping, lisping mimminee-pimminee'*—and assured his readers that:

> *There will also be found in these volumes little of what is usually called poetic diction; as much pains has been taken to avoid it as is ordinarily taken to produce it.*

Wordsworth has endeavoured to

> *imitate, and, as far as is possible, to adopt the very language of men,*

and in particular men of *'humble and rustic life'* because

> *such men hourly communicate with the best objects from which the best part of language is originally derived.*

23. *William Wordsworth* by B. R. Haydon. Wordsworth, whose ideas on poetic language seemed so revolutionary, is depicted here by Haydon as a staid Victorian gentleman—which, indeed, he had become, accepting the position of Poet Laureate in 1843. (National Portrait Gallery, London)

Such a radical and astonishing swing away from the concept of poetic diction was too much for many critics—even for Wordsworth's co-author of *Lyrical Ballads*, Samuel Taylor Coleridge, who felt that Wordsworth had perhaps gone too far. '*Little can I agree*', he wrote in *Biographia Literaria*,

> *with the assertion, that from the objects with which the rustic hourly communicates the best part of language is formed . . . The few things, and modes of action, requisite for his bodily*

conveniences, would alone be individualized . . . It is more than probable, that many classes of the brute creation possess discriminating sounds, by which they can convey to each other notices of such objects as concern their food, shelter and safety. Yet we hesitate to call the aggregate of such sounds a language, otherwise than metaphorically.[6]

Hazlitt, reflecting in 1818 on the Lake School of poets, also condemned the *'rustic'* approach: *'peasants, pedlars and village-barbers were their oracles and bosom friends'*, he jeered. Nevertheless, Hazlitt admitted that:

Our poetical literature had, towards the close of the last century, degenerated into the most trite, insipid, and mechanical of all things . . . It wanted something to stir it up.

But this is his main criticism of the Romantic poets: they have looked for something to *'stir it up'* and, being inspired by French Revolutionary tendencies, have merely aimed at novelty for its own sake:

all was to be natural and new . . . a classical allusion was considered as a piece of antiquated foppery . . . regular metre was abolished along with regular government . . . a striking effect . . . something new and original, no matter whether good, bad or indifferent . . . was all that was aimed at.

But Wordsworth's intention was decidedly *not* to aim at passing novelty; on the contrary, he wanted to develop a language which would derive permanent value from having arisen *'out of repeated experience and regular feelings'* as opposed to *'arbitrary and capricious habits of expression'*. Nor did he look only to *'something new and original'* as Hazlitt claimed; like many Romantic poets, Wordsworth looked back to the excellences of Chaucer, which he pointed out

are almost always expressed in language pure and universally intelligible even to this day.

This admiration for medieval and pre-eighteenth-century writers is partly, as we saw in Chapter 7, a symptom of the interest in all things Gothic as a reaction against eighteenth-century rationality. But it is also expressive of genuine interest in the development of language, and the search for what Coleridge, now praising Wordsworth, called *'a perfect appropriateness of the words to the meaning'*.

In an endeavour to reach this goal, Keats was consciously influenced by other, earlier poets, notably Spenser, Shakespeare and

24. *William Hazlitt* by William Bewick. The critic, Hazlitt, whose sharp observations on the literature of his time still seem fresh and lively today, was drawn by Bewick, the wood-engraver and friend of Haydon; Bewick's *Memoirs* reveal bitter criticism of contemporary society. (National Portrait Gallery, London)

Milton—and also by Chatterton, who lived not long before Keats, but who wrote in pseudo-medieval verse. Not all these influences were happy ones; Keats came to feel, for example, that the language of Milton was as guilty of *'poetic diction'* as the eighteenth-century style. Writing to George and Georgiana Keats in 1819, he explains that:

> *The Paradise lost though so fine in itself is a corruption of our*
> *Language—it should be kept as it is unique—a curiosity—a*
> *beautiful and grand Curiosity. The most remarkable Pro-*
> *duction of the world. A northern dialect accommodating itself*
> *to greek and latin inversions and intonations . . . I have but*
> *lately stood on my guard against Milton. Life to him would be*
> *death to me. Miltonic verse cannot be written but (in) the vein*
> *of art.*[7]

He had already made the same point to his friend Reynolds, explaining why he had given up his poem 'Hyperion':

> *there were too many Miltonic inversions in it—Miltonic verse*
> *can not be written but in an artful or rather artist's humour*
> *. . . English ought to be kept up. It may be interesting for you*
> *to pick out some lines from Hyperion and put a mark X to the*
> *false beauty proceeding from art, and one | | to the true voice of*
> *feeling.*[8]

However, a reading of 'Hyperion' by those acquainted with *Paradise
Lost* will quickly reveal that Keats has not only used *'Miltonic
inversions'*, but that he has put them to good effect; he has, in fact,
learnt Milton's trick of turning a phrase so that the heavy emphasis
of the beat falls on a particular word. For example, in the description
of Hyperion himself, we read:

> *At this, through all his bulk an agony*
> *Crept gradual, from the feet unto the crown*[9]

where *'gradual'* is strongly marked because of its position. Later,
Enceladus is described as having

> *A pallid gleam across his features stern,*[10]

where *'stern'*, though out of its natural order, gains a heavy emphasis
through falling on the final monosyllable—a technique much used
by Milton.

The Romantic poets, then, were not merely seeking novelty in
their style. They were genuinely interested in how they used
language to express their ideas; and because their ideas were different from those of previous writers, their style often needed to be too.
Keats, for example, was concerned with *'sensations rather than . . .
thoughts'*. So, when he wishes to convey ideas, he generally approaches
our minds through our senses. To see this technique in full opera-
tion, we have only to examine 'The Eve of St Agnes'. Keats wishes

to show that Madeline is chaste and pure; to do so, he does not state the fact explicitly. Instead, and more tellingly, he uses the sensation of coldness proverbially associated with chastity (cf. Othello to the dead Desdemona: *'Cold, cold my girl! Even like thy chastity!'*) It is a *'wintry day'*, and Madeline's chamber is lit by a *'wintry moon'* (itself the sign of Diana, goddess of Chastity). Her bed is a *'chilly nest'*, where the linen is *'blanched'*; the chamber is a *'chilly room'*, and her dream is *'Impossible to melt as iced stream'*. Porphyro, on the contrary, is *'on fire'* with love and the thought of Madeline comes *'Flushing his brow'*; once in her room his arm is *'warm'*, and when she speaks he becomes *'Ethereal, flushed, and like a throbbing star'*, so that he *'melted'* into her dream.

Sensation—this time of taste—is also used by Keats in the sumptuous feasts which seem to have symbolic significance for him, and to represent some kind of solemn ceremonial turning-point. Porphyro spreads a feast for Madeline; Lycius gives one in Lamia's palace; the poet in 'Fall of Hyperion' finds one in the temple. In each case, the feast is the prelude to some momentous development, some changed state of *mind* which Keats makes us feel by attacking our *senses* with his *'lucent syrops'*, *'wine . . . from the gloomy tun'* and *'feast of summer fruits'*.

Shelley also found that he could best depict *'the operations of the human mind'* indirectly, through imagery, as he explicitly states in his preface to *Prometheus Unbound*. So, in that poem, as in *Hellas*, physical revolt and suffering are used by Shelley to depict mental attitudes to tyranny. Equally, poems such as 'Ode to the West Wind' or 'The Cloud' use changes in natural objects to suggest changes in human history.

As Shelley was particularly concerned to question existing values, it is perhaps not surprising that one of his most interesting uses of language is to startle his readers into new awareness by a complete breakaway from conventional imagery. In *A Defence of Poetry*, he claims this as a function of poets, whose *'language is vitally metaphorical; that is, it marks the before unapprehended relation of things.'* So, in 'The Revolt of Islam', the eagle, accepted Christian symbol of aspiration to God, is the personification of evil, while the serpent, the mythological, Biblical, and hence traditional, symbol of evil, becomes the symbol of good, wretchedly changed *'from starry shape, beauteous and mild'*. Similarly, Shelley changes word-values. *'Faith'*, far from being an inspiration to good, acquires an almost obscene meaning. It is *'monstrous'*, allied with *'Plague and slaughter'*—for to Shelley it implies the unquestioning acceptance of corrupt customs.

So, too, kings are described as *'slaves'*, and God as a false creation of man.

Shelley also pushes us to a greater awareness by putting together apparent incompatibles and hence making us perceive new relationships. Indeed, he sees this as a major function of poetry, which *'marries exultation and horror, grief and pleasure, eternity and change; it subdues to union, under its light yoke, all irreconcilable things'*. So, in 'A Vision of the Sea', the waves are impossibly described as *'flames'*, or *'whirlpools of fire-flowing iron'*. In *Prometheus Unbound*, the chariot seen by Ione is described as having wheels like *'solid clouds'*. In 'The Cloud', Shelley suggests its enduring quality by the outrageous device of repeatedly using solid imagery which is totally inappropriate to something nebulous:

> *'the* towers *of my skiey bowers'*
> *'in a* cavern *under is* fettered *the thunder'*
> *'my fleece-like* floor*'*
> *'a* bridge-*like shape'*
> *'I hang like a* roof*'*
> *'the* pavilion *of Heaven'*
> *'the blue* dome *of air'.*

He also delights in paradox, as in his poem 'On the Medusa of Leonardo Da Vinci', whose loveliness is

> *like a* shadow, *from which* shine . . .
> *The agonies of anguish and of death,*

and whose *'grace'*, ironically, since it is a statue, *'turns the gazer's spirit into stone'*.

This new awareness of the possibility of using language to attack the emotions and the senses, and thus to influence the mind, is central to Romanticism. Rather than argue us into seeing their point of view, the Romantic poets wish to make us feel their sensations and hence to sympathize—in the full sense of that word—with their aims. They have a right and a duty to seek to influence us in this way, being *'institutors of laws and the founders of civil society'*, *'legislators or prophets'*, and they also know that the poet is

> *endowed with more lively sensibility, more enthusiasm and tenderness . . . a greater knowledge of human nature, and a more comprehensive soul*[11]

than the majority of men. Language is the means by which the poet fulfils his responsibilities; it is a precious gift given only to a few. For

> *every man whose soul is not a clod*
> *Hath visions, and would speak, if he had lov'd,*
> *And been well nurtured in his mother tongue.*[12]

But not every man has that ability:

> *For Poesy alone can tell her dreams.*[13]

[1] Lord Chesterfield *Letters of Lord Chesterfield to His Son and Others* (Dent, 1935) p. 2   [2] Samuel Johnson (ed. by M. Wilson) *Prose and Poetry* (Hart-Davis, 1963) p. 860   [3] *ibid.* p. 301   [4] *ibid.* p. 301   [5] *ibid.* p. 319   [6] S. T. Coleridge (ed. by Shawcross) *Biographia Literaria* (vol. 2) (O.U.P., 1939) p. 39   [7] K.L. p. 341   [8] *ibid.* p. 327   [9] 'Hyperion' Book I, 259-60   [10] *ibid.* Book II, 349   [11] William Wordsworth 'Preface to Lyrical Ballads'   [12] J. Keats 'Fall of Hyperion' 13-15   [13] *ibid.* 8

10

The Influence of Greece and Italy

Since the eighteenth century owed so much to classical antiquity, and since the Romantic movement was in many respects a revolt against that allegiance, we should expect the English Romantic poets to reject any association with the culture of Greece and Rome. And to a certain extent this was true of the early Romantic writers. Mythology, for example, is not much evident in Wordsworth. But for the later Romantic poets, such as Keats and Shelley, Greece and Italy, both of classical and contemporary times, were of the utmost importance.

Shelley, of course, spent the last four years of his life in Italy. Keats arrived in time to die there. But for both poets, their interest in Italy and Greece was a long-standing one. More, it was a vital intense experience, deliberately sought and delightedly pursued throughout adult life. And, as one might expect, such a deep-seated influence had an immediate effect on their writing.

A basic and obvious example is the widespread use of classical mythology which at once strikes the reader of Keats' poetry. 'Endymion', 'Hyperion', 'Lamia', 'Fall of Hyperion', 'Ode to Psyche'—all these exhibit the kind of detailed knowledge of mythological characters which Keats had assiduously gleaned since his school days, from such works as Lemprière's popular *Classical Dictionary*, published in 1788. Myth seems to have been particularly attractive to Keats, perhaps because it is so often a condensation into the form of a particular story of a general truth about human nature, human experience or human history. As such, it would fit perfectly with Keats' instinctive use of individual experience to express universal truth. There is also, of course, the convenient fact that most of his audience would at least recognize the more obvious characters—would know, for example, that Apollo was god of poetry. This enables Keats to use Apollo as a recurrent and easily understood image in poems which explore his own desire to achieve poetic excellence. So we have the early 'Ode to Apollo', 'Apollo to the Graces', and the apologetic 'Hymn of Apollo'. And in 'Hyperion' and 'The Fall of Hyperion' we quickly understand the full signific-

25. *San Giorgio from the Dogana, Venice* by J. M. W. Turner. The strange, fascinating beauty of Venice is exactly captured by Turner in this evocative watercolour. (The British Museum, London)

ance of Apollo's music, *'Like pearl beads dropping sudden from their string'*, to one who so greatly desired to be *'among the English Poets after my death.'*

The other influence which Keats specifically celebrates in his poetry is that of Homer. His introduction to Chapman's translation seemed to Keats like a thrilling awakening of the soul—a moment of discovery and inspiration which he captured in sonnet form in 'On First Looking into Chapman's Homer':

> *Then felt I like some watcher of the skies*
> *When a new planet swims into his ken;*
> *Or like stout Cortez when with eagle eyes*
> *He star'd at the Pacific—and all his men*
> *Look'd at each other with a wild surmise,*
> *Silent, upon a peak in Darien.*

The legend that Homer was blind—like Milton, another writer greatly admired by Keats—also moved him deeply. To one who felt that the realm of imagination could be more real than observable fact, the idea of a blind poet, forced to dwell with internal truth alone, must have been an extremely powerful image. It was one which Milton himself had come to terms with in 'Samson Agonistes'. Keats briefly explores the same theme in his sonnet 'To Homer':

Aye, on the shores of darkness there is light,
And precipices show untrodden green;
There is a budding morrow in midnight;
There is a triple sight in blindness keen;

Shelley, too, had more than a passing knowledge of classical antiquity. Not only was he a keen student of Gibbon's *Decline and Fall of the Roman Empire*; he had read widely in classical literature, forging through, among others, the works of Lucretius, Plutarch, Plato, Homer and the dramatists Aeschylus, Euripides and Sophocles. He, too, made some use of myth and, like Keats, used Apollo to remind us of the divine nature of the poet. But Shelley's Apollo, of course, is a poet and lawgiver, prophet and reformer:

The sunbeams are my shafts, with which I kill
Deceit, that loves the night and fears the day;
All men who do or ever imagine ill
Fly me, and from the glory of my ray
Good minds and open actions take new might,
Until diminished by the reign of Night.[1]

Predictably, the works of ancient writers which have most overt influence on Shelley are those which reflect his favourite theories. One can imagine the delight with which he must have studied Aeschylus' treatment of the Prometheus myth, and the attack on the cruelty of Zeus, the absolute monarch. Aeschylus depicts Prometheus doomed to ages of torment because he would not

accept the sovereignty of Zeus
And cease acting as champion of the human race.

Zeus is '*hard to appease*', ruling '*tyranically*', but even he will, of necessity, be overthrown one day, for '*He cannot fly from fate*'; he will learn '*how great a chasm lies between ruling and being ruled.*' Meanwhile, the task of the hero of humanity is to stay firm.

I would not change my painful plight
On any terms, for your servile humility,

he announces with dignity, anticipating the Shelleyan stand against established authority. The reader of Aeschylus can immediately see the attraction which the play must have held for Shelley—and yet Shelley had some reservations. He takes pains to point out to his audience that he was not merely attempting to restore the lost sequel of Aeschylus' play (which was written as part of a trilogy). For Aeschylus, the sequel to Prometheus' sufferings was his eventual reconciliation with Jupiter; to Shelley, this was unsatisfactory, as he explains clearly in his Preface:

> *Had I framed my story on this model, I should have done no more than have attempted to restore the lost drama of Aeschylus . . . But, in truth, I was averse from a catastrophe so feeble as that of reconciling the champion with the Oppressor of mankind. The moral interest of the fable, which is so powerfully sustained by the sufferings and endurance of Prometheus, would be annihilated if we could conceive of him as unsaying his high language and quailing before his successful and perfidious adversary.*

In the same year that he finished *Prometheus*, Shelley translated another ancient drama with the same basic theme—the solitary hero standing out against the tyrant. This was *The Cyclops* by Euripides, where Ulysses is trapped by the inhospitable and vicious Polyphemus, but escapes by playing on the baser instincts of the giant, getting him drunk, and blinding him.

What Shelley so admired in Aeschylus' and Euripides' plays— a celebration of individual justice and freedom against tyranny— was at the root of his admiration for the whole Grecian civilization. At its most glorious (roughly in the fifth century B.C.) and in its most famous city, Athens, Greek political and cultural life had achieved what Shelley—and many others—saw as an ideal. In particular, Athens operated a working democracy, in which every adult male citizen had a voice. It was not a perfect society; but, as Shelley asserts in his 'On the Manners of the Ancient Greeks', it created excellence in every sphere of life:

> *The period which intervenes between the birth of Pericles and the death of Aristotle is undoubtedly . . . the most memorable in the history of the world . . . which produced so unparalleled a progress during that period in literature and the arts . . . Their sculptures are such as we in our presumption assume to be the models of ideal truth and beauty.*

This was, for Shelley, the perfect society—one in which political freedom and artistic excellence went hand in hand, reinforcing and recreating each other. And though in changed conditions it might now be only a dream, men could point to Athens as proof that it had once existed.

Ancient Athens, then, was an example to look back on; but more importantly, it also represented an inspiration to the present. Another of Aeschylus' plays, *The Persians*, gave nineteenth-century reformers and revolutionaries the encouraging lesson that superior forces and established empire might be overthrown by courage and determination. Aeschylus' play celebrates the defeat of the mighty Persian forces by the Athenians at Salamis in 480 B.C., and in so doing celebrates the triumph of democracy over tyranny. As H. D. F. Kitto explains in his book *The Greeks*:

> *The Greeks had always thought fairly well of themselves, in comparison with 'barbarians': that impression was confirmed. They had always thought that their free institutions were better than Oriental despotisms: events proved that they were right. The Asiatic master compelled obedience by torture and the lash: the Greeks took their decisions by debating and persuading—and then acted like one man: and they conquered. No wonder that the next generation filled its temple-pediments with sculptured representations of the old mythical battle between the earth-born Giants and the Olympian Gods. The Greek Gods had triumphed again, freedom and reason had defeated despotism and fear.*

The play was thus of general interest to Shelley; it became of particular significance when the Greek Revolt broke out against detail later in this chapter, led Shelley to write *Hellas*, directly inspired by *The Persians*, which, he says, '*afforded me the first model of my conception*'. In his Preface to *Hellas*, Shelley sums up civilization's debt to ancient Greece:

> *We are all Greeks. Our laws, our literature, our religion, our arts have their root in Greece. But for Greece—Rome, the instructor, the conqueror, or the metropolis of our ancestors, would have spread no illumination with her arms, and we might still have been savages and idolators . . .*
>
> *The human form and the human mind attained to a perfection in Greece which has impressed its image on those faultless productions, whose very fragments are the despair of modern art, and has propagated impulses which cannot cease, through a thousand channels of manifest or imperceptible operation, to ennoble and delight mankind until the extinction of the race.*

Further evidence that, to Shelley and his followers, the civilization of ancient Athens—and of ancient Rome at its best—was a model of the noblest life for all time, can be found, perhaps surprisingly, in Mary Shelley's *Frankenstein*, where one of the three works with which the 'monster' educates himself is Plutarch's *Lives* (a favourite with Shelley himself). The 'monster' says:

> *Plutarch taught me high thoughts; he elevated me above the wretched sphere of my own reflections, to admire and love the heroes of past ages . . . I read of men concerned in public affairs, governing or massacring their species. I felt the greatest ardour for virtue rise within me, and abhorrence for vice . . . Induced by these feelings, I was of course led to admire peaceable lawgivers, Numa, Solon, and Lycurgus, in preference to Romulus and Theseus.*

The lives of past democrats were, to Shelley and his family, an ideal to compare with past—and present—tyrants.

If Shelley felt a debt to ancient Greece in general, it is apparent that he owes an especial debt to one Greek in particular—Plato. The Platonic conception of the ideal, the absolute—that is, that the objects perceived by our senses are only shadows of an ultimate, unchanging reality—is very dear to Shelley's heart. The recurrent theme in Shelley of the search for ideal love or beauty is an echo of the *Symposium* of Plato (which, incidentally, Shelley himself translated). The millennium, the new Hellas, which Shelley looks forward to, is an embodiment of this perfection, which Plato, writing as Socrates, describes as:

> *absolute, existing alone with itself, unique, eternal and all other beautiful things as partaking of it.*

It is a self-evident truth, says Socrates, that the seeker is not in possession of such beauty, or he would have no need to seek it; so Shelley, in 'The Sensitive Plant', describes how

> *the Sensitive Plant has no bright flower;*
> *Radiance and odour are not its dower;*
> *It loves, even like Love, its deep heart is full,*
> *It desires what it has not, the Beautiful!*[2]

So, over and over again in Shelley's poetry, we see his heroes and heroines searching for *'beautiful idealisms of moral excellence'*. They may not find them, but Shelley feels the quest for perfection is worth while. He would rather *'be damned with Plato'* than *'go to Heaven with . . . Malthus'*.

*   *   *

If the literature of the ancient Greeks was vital to Keats and Shelley, that of the medieval Italian writers was also important. Tasso, Ariosto and Petrarch were all of some significance to the Romantic poets; and we have seen (Chapter 7) how Boccaccio exerted his influence on Keats. But the most important medieval Italian writer, for both Keats and Shelley, was Dante. Dante Alighieri (1265–1321) was born in Florence. He is most widely known for his work, *The Divine Comedy*, in which the poet Virgil conducts him through Hell and Purgatory to Paradise, where Dante meets Beatrice, the lady, now dead, whom he passionately loved and whom he now sees as his *'beatitude'*, his hope of salvation. For Shelley, one suspects that the attraction was partly this view of Beatrice as an ideal, inspiring love, reflecting his ideas about a search after absolute perfection which, as we have noted, he also drew from Plato. Shelley was also attracted, however, by the vitality and beauty of Dante's mind, which he felt outshone even the greatest of the ancient writers:

> *Perhaps Dante created imaginations of greater loveliness and energy than any that are to be found in the ancient literature of Greece.*[3]

He may have produced a *'misty ocean of . . . dark and extravagant fiction'*, but it is studded with *'fortunate isles laden with golden fruit'*. Moreover, Dante gave new life to European literature:

> *Dante was the first awakener of entranced Europe; he created a language, in itself music and persuasion, out of a chaos of inharmonious barbarisms. He was . . . the Lucifer of that starry flock which in the thirteenth century shone from republican Italy, as from a heaven into the darkness of the benighted world.*[4]

It is perhaps typical of their different attitudes that Shelley should celebrate Dante's impact on civilization, while Keats is intensely concerned with the impression produced on his own imagination. His passionate interest in *The Divine Comedy* is shown by the fact that the only books he took on his northern walking tour were the *'three little Volumes'* of Dante recently translated (1805–14) by Henry Cary. The following spring he dreamt of an incident in the *Inferno* (the first part of *The Divine Comedy*) concerning the lovers Paulo and Francesca:

26. *Dante and Virgil Approaching the Angel Who Guards the Entrance to Purgatory*
by William Blake. Dante inspired many artists and writers, but his vision is
changed by Blake, who sees the angel as representative of a harsh, forbidding
religion (Tate Gallery, London)

> *The dream was one of the most delightful enjoyments I ever had in my life—I floated about the whirling atmosphere as it is described with a beautiful figure to whose lips mine were joined ... for an age—and in the midst of all this cold and darkness I was warm—even flowery tree tops sprung up and we rested on them sometimes with the lightness of a cloud till the wind blew us away again—I tried a sonnet upon it—there are fourteen lines but nothing of what I felt in it—O that I could dream it every night ...* [5]

(The sonnet, interestingly, expends its first eight lines, not in references to Dante, but to characters and places of Greek mythology—Hermes, Argus, Jove, Delphi, Ida and Tempe.) Keats' interest in Dante grew, and was a major motive in his decision to learn Italian. *'I like to be acquainted with foreign languages'*, he wrote to his brother George. *'Also the reading of Dante* (is) *well worth the while.'*

*   *   *

But it would be quite wrong to give the impression that reading, however *'well worth the while'*, was the only or even the major source of acquaintance which Keats and Shelley had with the culture of Italy and Greece. Keats never set foot in Greece, never visited the ruins of the ancient civilizations; even so, in 1817, he had a chance to see the best of Greek art, when his friend, the artist Robert Haydon, took him to see the Elgin Marbles.

These were sculptures, originally decorating the Parthenon in Athens, which Lord Elgin brought back to England (rightly or wrongly; the point was hotly debated). Haydon himself recalls in his *Autobiography* the moment when he first saw them—and in so doing gives us an insight into the Romantic artist's striving after Nature:

> *The first thing I fixed my eyes on was the wrist of a figure in one of the female groups, in which were visible ... the radius and ulna. I was astonished, for I had never seen them hinted at in any female wrist in the antique ... That combination of nature and idea which I had felt was so much wanting for high art was here displayed ... My heart beat! If I had seen nothing else I had beheld sufficient to keep me to nature for the rest of my life ... I saw, in fact, the most heroic style of art combined with all the essential detail of actual life.*

Haydon communicated his enthusiasm to Keats, and took him along

to see the Marbles. Keats was overwhelmed. Like his introduction
to Chapman's Homer, it was a thrilling yet humbling experience,
and one which was to implant in him the conviction that beauty and
eternal truth go hand in hand (a conviction most pithily summed up
in the Ode celebrating another form of Attic art—the Grecian Urn).
To see the Elgin Marbles was such a wonderful mental experience
as to be almost physically painful. As he says in 'On Seeing the Elgin
Marbles':

> *Such dim-conceived glories of the brain*
> *Bring round the heart an indescribable feud;*
> *So do these wonders a most dizzy pain,*
> *That mingles Grecian grandeur with the rude*
> *Wasting of old Time—with a billowy main—*
> *A sun—a shadow of a magnitude.*

It may well have been the impression made on him by these
sculptures at the start of his poetic career which produced in Keats'
poetry the recurring impression that figures are like statues, frozen
solid, immobile. There is a sense of it in 'Endymion', where the hero
and Peona sit, silent, brooding over his troubles; but it becomes
progressively more apparent as his work matures. So in 'Hyperion',
Saturn is like a carved rock, *'gray-hair'd . . . quiet as a stone, still.'*
His hand is *'nerveless, listless, dead, Unsceptred'*. When Thea comes,
she kneels down beside him, and stays *'postured motionless, Like
natural sculpture in cathedral cavern'*. In complete contrast to this
picture of carved stone, Hyperion's palace is seen in images of
molten, flowing metal, and flashing light—*'glowing gold'*, *'fiery
galleries'*, *'poisonous brass'*, *'diamond-paved lustrous long arcades'*,
'crystalline pavilions'. But when we return to the Titans, we are back
to sculptured stone:

> *Crag jutting forth to crag, and rocks that seem'd*
> *Ever as if just rising from a sleep . . .*
> *Instead of thrones, hard flint they sat upon,*
> *Couches of rugged stone . . .*
> *Dungeon'd in opaque element, to keep*
> *Their clenched teeth still clench'd, and all their limbs . . .*
> *Without a motion . . .*
> > *. . . like a dismal cirque*
> *Of Druid stones.*[6]

So, too, in 'The Eve of St Agnes', the contrast with the *'argent
revelry'* is made, not only by the cold of the night and the solemn

prayers of the Beadsman, but by the motionless quality of the *'sculptur'd dead'* which

> *seem to freeze*
> *Emprison'd in black, purgatorial rails.*[7]

And when Madeline opens her eyes and sees Porphyro, we are made fully aware of the silence and tension as he waits to see how she will react, for this fiery youth, who until now has been constantly associated with images of heat and colour, becomes *'pale as smooth-sculptured stone'*. A similar experience strikes the poet himself in 'The Fall of Hyperion', when he is almost literally *'petrified'* during his effort to climb the temple steps:

> *Slow, heavy, deadly was my pace: the cold*
> *Grew stifling, suffocating, at the heart;*
> *And when I clasp'd my hands I felt them not.*[8]

And of course the picture of the fallen Saturn is repeated from the earlier 'Hyperion'.

For Shelley, knowledge of ancient sculpture and architecture had more immediacy, for he spent the last few years of his life travelling amongst it. He found the ruined buildings singularly impressive, especially the Coliseum, which, he wrote to Peacock,

> *is of enormous height and circuit, and the arches built of massy*
> *stones are piled on one another, and jut into the blue air,*
> *shattered into the forms of overhanging rocks.*[9]

Elsewhere he writes of the beauty of the decorative carving and the *'fragments of capitals and cornice, fretted with delicate sculptures'.* But Shelley, we must remember, was also a political animal, and he saw also that ancient beauty could be, as in Rome, a cover for ancient tyranny:

> *Solemn temples, where the Senate of the world assembled,*
> *palaces, triumphal arches, and cloud-surrounded columns . . .*
> *what actions and deliberations have they been destined to*
> *enclose and commemorate? Superstitious rites . . . schemes for*
> *wide-extended murder, and devastation, and misrule, and*
> *servitude.*[10]

In fact, what seems to have impressed Shelley most was not what survived, but how, like the statue of Ozymandias, these mighty works had fallen, to succumb to the eternal movements of nature. *'It has been changed by times,'* he wrote to Peacock of the Coliseum,

> *into the image of an amphitheatre of rocky hills, overgrown by*
> *the wild olive, the myrtle and the fig-tree, and threaded by*
> *little paths which wind among its ruined stairs and immeasur-*
> *able galleries.*[11]

He summed his view up in a three-line fragment written in 1819:

> *Rome has fallen, ye see it lying*
> *Heaped in undistinguished ruin;*
> *Nature is alone undying.*

While the monuments of ancient Italy were a reminder of past
tyrannies, Italy of the early nineteenth century had an immediate
impact on him. In one sense, it was naturally a tragic influence,
since two of the Shelley children died during these four years in
Italy. And yet, simultaneously, it was a source of great poetic
vitality. Shelley never hesitated to acknowledge that the Italian
climate and scenery were responsible for a new vigour in his work.
In his Preface to *Prometheus Unbound*, he describes how

> *This Poem was chiefly written upon the mountainous ruins of*
> *the Baths of Caracalla, among the flowery glades, and*
> *thickets of odoriferous blossoming trees, which are extended in*
> *ever winding labyrinths upon its immense platforms and*
> *dizzy arches suspended in the air. The bright blue sky of*
> *Rome, and the effect of the vigorous awakening spring in that*
> *divinest climate, and the new life with which it drenches the*
> *spirits even to intoxication, were the inspiration of this drama.*

In her note on *The Cenci*, Mary Shelley describes how her husband
was invigorated, even after the death of the beloved eldest child, by
the changes in weather, and the Italian sun:

> *Sometimes, the dark lurid clouds dipped towards the waves,*
> *and became waterspouts that churned up the water beneath . . .*
> *At other times, the dazzling sunlight and heat made it almost*
> *intolerable to every other, but Shelley basked in both and his*
> *health and spirits revived under their influence.*

The scenery, too, dazzled him, and inspired many of his later poems,
such as 'Lines Written among the Euganean Hills', where, in
particular, the beauty of Venice attracts him, thrown into vivid
silhouette by the sun:

> *And before that chasm of light,*
> *As within a furnace bright,*

Column, tower, and dome, and spire,
Shine like obelisks of fire,
Pointing with inconstant motion
From the altar of dark ocean
To the sapphire-tinted skies;[12]

(In true Shelleyan fashion, the beauty only serves to remind the poet of hidden corruption.)

And it was a visit to Lord Byron at Venice (*'he took me in his gondola ... When we disembarked ... we rode along the sands'*) which inspired the poem 'Julian and Maddalo', which begins with a description of the Venetian shore:

a bare strand
Of hillocks, heaped from ever-shifting sand
Matted with thistles and amphibious weeds,
Such as from earth's embrace the salt ooze breeds,
Is this; an uninhabited sea-side,
Which the lone fisher, when his nets are dried,
Abandons; ...
This ride was my delight. I love all waste
And solitary places; ...
... the winds drove
The living spray along the sunny air
Into our faces, the blue heavens were bare ...
And from the waves, sound like delight broke forth

But if Shelley could soak in the Italian sun, and draw upon Italian scenery for inspiration, this did not mean that Keats, locked in a gloomier northern climate, could not share something of the same pleasures. Certainly they were delights he longed for: in the winter of 1816, much as he enjoys English scenery and admires English women, he does

sometimes feel a languishment
For skies Italian, and an inward groan
To sit upon an Alp as on a throne ...
... often warmly burn to see
Beauties of deeper glance, and hear their singing
And float with them about the summer waters![13]

It was something he must have felt deeply at such times as his stay in Devonshire in early 1818, when the rain poured down, and he was compelled to describe it as a *'splashy, rainy, misty, snowy, foggy, haily, floody, muddy, slipshod county.'*

Deprived of the Italian sunshine for which he longed, Keats

seems to have invented it for himself. His poems are aglow with
a conscious delight in warm, rich colour. Partly, of course, this is an
inheritance from Spenser—his early 'Imitation of Spenser' can
scarcely move a line without at least one adjective of colour, often
more. But it is also an attempt to bring to his poems the dazzling
effects of Italian light and colour which were to be so brilliantly
captured later by the paintings of Turner. So, in 'Hyperion', Keats'
invocation to the Muse is a prayer rich in colour and warmth (or
the delicious contrasting iciness of cooled wine) and luxurious
growth:

> Flush everything that hath a vermeil hue,
> Let the rose glow intense and warm the air,
> And let the clouds of even and of morn
> Float in voluptuous fleeces o'er the hills;
> Let the red wine within the goblet boil,
> Cold as a bubbling well; let faint-lipp'd shells,
> On sands, or in great deeps, vermilion turn
> Through all their labyrinths; and let the maid
> Blush keenly, as with some warm kiss surprised.
> Chief isle of the embowered Cyclades,
> Rejoice, O Delos, with thine olive green,
> And poplars, and lawn-shading palms, and beech . . .
> And hazels thick, dark-stemm'd beneath the shade.[14]

*   *   *

Although Keats could, through imagination, share with Shelley
the scenery and warmth of a glowing southern climate, there was
one aspect of contemporary life in Greece and Italy which Keats
did not live to see, which to Shelley was of paramount importance.
This was a sudden outburst, in 1821, in the struggle for freedom and
independence in both Italy and Greece. Italy at this time was divided
into a number of states, none of great power, and many under the
domination of Austria, while Greece was subjected to the harsh
rule of the Ottoman Turks. Mary Shelley reviews the situation in
her 'Note on *Hellas*':

> The South of Europe was in a state of great political excitement
> at the beginning of the year 1821 . . . when Naples rose to
> declare the Constitution, the call was responded to from
> Brindisium to the foot of the Alps. To crush these attempts to
> obtain liberty, early in 1821, the Austrians poured their
> armies into the Peninsula; at first their coming rather seemed

> *to add energy and resolution to a people long enslaved. The*
> *Piedmontese asserted their freedom; Genoa threw off the yoke*
> *of the King of Sardinia; and, as if in playful imitation, the*
> *people of the little state of Massa and Carrara gave the*
> *'congé' to their sovereign, and set up a republic. . . .*
>
> *Shelley, as well as every other lover of liberty, looked upon*
> *the struggles . . . as decisive of the destinies of the world,*
> *probably for centuries to come. The interest he took in the*
> *progress of affairs was intense . . . Day after day he read the*
> *bulletins of the Austrian army, and sought eagerly to gather*
> *tokens of its defeat . . . His whole heart and soul were in the*
> *triumph of the cause . . . While the fate of the progress of the*
> *Austrian armies then invading Naples was yet in suspense, the*
> *news of another revolution filled him with exultation.*

This new revolution was the outbreak of the Greek War of Independence against their Turkish overlords. As we saw earlier in this chapter, it inspired his work *Hellas*, based on a similar Greek attack on Eastern tyranny over two thousand years before. Once again, he felt, Greece, from which we all drew our civilization, would show the way to freedom. (Nor was Shelley the only Romantic poet who felt like this. In 1823 Byron set off to fight for the Greek cause, and died of fever at Missolonghi the following year.) That Shelley indeed saw Athens as a symbol of the new world which was to come is obvious, both from *Hellas* itself, and from the earlier 'Ode to Liberty' where he sees the *'bards and sages'* of Athens still influencing the movement towards freedom:

> *A wingèd sound of joy, and love, and wonder,*
> *Which soars where expectation never flew,*
> *Rending the veil of space and time asunder!*[15]

A new Greece, a new Italy, a new world would come—some day.

*   *   *

Shelley did not live to see either Greece or Italy emerge from its political struggles. And Keats had died a year before him. But Shelley had already left his own epitaph in the elegy he wrote for Keats—'Adonais'. Both poets were buried in Rome, the symbol for Shelley of decayed glory and ruined empire which the eternal truth of the poet can outlive:

> *Or go to Rome, which is the sepulchre,*
> *Oh, not of him, but of our joy: 'tis nought*

27. *Lord Byron* by T. Phillips. Lord Byron, like Shelley, lived in Italy in an exile partly self-imposed and partly necessitated by scandal. He fervently embraced the Greek cause against the Turks. (National Portrait Gallery, London)

> *That ages, empires, and religions there*
> *Lie buried in the ravage they have wrought;*
> *For such as he can lend—they borrow not*
> *Glory from those who made the world their prey;*
> *And he is gathered to the kings of thought*
> *Who waged contention with their time's decay,*
> *And of the past are all that cannot pass away.*[16]

[1] 'Hymn of Apollo' 13–19   [2] 'The Sensitive Plant' Part I, 74–7
[3] A. S. B. Glover (ed.) *Shelley, Selected Poetry, Prose and Letters*
(Nonesuch Press, 1951) p. 1017   [4] *ibid.* pp. 1045–6   [5] K. L. p. 278
[6] 'Hyperion' Book II, 10–11; 15–16; 23–4; 26; 34–5   [7] 'The Eve of
St Agnes' II, 5–6   [8] 'The Fall of Hyperion' 129–31   [9] as 3, p. 1082
[10] D. L. Clark (ed.) *Shelley's Prose* (University of New Mexico Press,
1954) p. 226   [11] as 3, p. 1082   [12] 'Lines Written Among the Euganean
Hills' 104–110   [13] J. Keats 'Happy Is England' 5–7, 12–14   [14] 'Hyperion' Book III, 14–25; 27   [15] 'Ode to Liberty' VI, 84–6   [16] 'Adonais'
XLVIII, 424–432

II

Reflections of the Spirit of the Age in Science, Music and Painting

As will have become evident throughout this book, Romanticism was not merely a literary movement. It was a whole way of seeing and responding to life, in its political, social and artistic fields. What began as a reaction to Classicism became in its own right a positive, driving force for enlarging all areas of the mind— much like the Renaissance of the fifteenth and sixteenth centuries.

In its sense of uncertainty, its questioning of established values, its interest in the unknown and irrational, the Romantic movement is still with us today. Science fiction is the new Gothic novel; the craze for antiques—indeed for anything different from modern regimented styles of building and furniture—replaces the taste for medievalism; and the rebelliousness of the younger generation reflected so completely in Shelley has been exhibited in recent years in such groups as the Flower People and the Hippies. The disenchantment with established religion continues too, and the search to put something in its place has moved beyond both Methodism and Shelleyan atheism to an interest in transcendental meditation. Like Beckford and the Prince Regent, modern Romantics look to the East for an answer.

At the end of the eighteenth century, as now, there was dissatisfaction with what Shelley called *'Society as it is'*; the human condition seemed restricted and confined. Keats and Shelley, like many other writers, saw greater intellectual freedom, brought about by increased knowledge, as one of the prerequisites of an improved life for humanity in general. So in literature, as we have seen, the age celebrated men like Faust, Manfred and Frankenstein, who soared beyond the bounds of human knowledge and custom. In real life, an attempt to gather together all knowledge had been made in the mid-eighteenth century by the French encyclopedists, whose monumental work, largely organized by the philosopher and critic Diderot, was condemned by the authorities in 1746, and burned.

Nevertheless, the idea of intellectual liberty grew with the movements for political and individual liberty at the end of the

century, and in the world of science the three seemed often to go hand in hand. Joseph Priestley, for example, the Unitarian minister who, as a Dissenter, had been barred from the Universities, showed that a mind untrammelled by prejudice could have much to offer. In 1767 he published a *History of Electricity* and, more importantly, in 1774 he discovered oxygen. However, Priestley's unorthodox religious views and his known support for the rebellious American colonists drew on him the anger of a 'Church and King' mob, which, on Bastille Day in the fearful, anti-revolutionary year of 1791 destroyed his house and library in Birmingham and drove him to finish his days in exile in America.

It was an American, Benjamin Franklin, who had suggested to Priestley that he should publish the *History of Electricity*, and Franklin is another example of the spirit of liberty and enquiry which is so representative of this age. An atheist, and an ardent supporter of the freedom of the thirteen colonies, Franklin was also a keen amateur scientist, and after various experiments with electricity, his speculation that lightning might be an electric charge led to his invention of the lightning conductor.

This kind of amateur passion for scientific inquiry, going hand in hand with an attitude of disrespect for existing institutions, can be found over and over again in the Romantic era—not least in Shelley himself, whose early experiments with the new, exciting and powerful force of electricity so terrified his sisters. Indeed, electricity became of symbolic significance for Shelley, standing as a kind of elemental or Promethean fire, as Richard Holmes explains in *Shelley—The Pursuit*. Referring to Shelley's comment on existing society in the Preface of *Prometheus Unbound* that

> *The cloud of mind is discharging its collected lightning, and the equilibrium between institutions and opinions is now restoring, or is about to be restored,*

Holmes remarks that *'The use of the electrical image, even here in the preface, was not coincidental in a drama about Prometheus, the fire-bringer'* and goes on to explain that when Shelley writes Panthea's description of the *'delicate spirit'*, the light that

> *floats along the spray of the salt sea*
> *Or makes its chariot of a foggy cloud*

he is in fact talking about electricity:

> *Electricity as the new fire satisfied the extension of the plot*

> *both mythically and scientifically. Electricity would be the great new power source to liberate man from physical servitude.*

It was a vision shared by others. Robert Owen was later to see electricity as an instrument for universal harmony:

> *the family of man may become one in interest, language and feeling, over the earth—this being now the evident ultimate object of society, and the means to hasten it being accomplished by the discovery of the electric telegraph.*

Another area in which science and the Romantic movement went hand in hand was geology. As the taste for wild scenery and rocky landscapes grew, so did the taste for fossils and the study of rock structures—though, ironically, geological knowledge was given an equally great boost by the industrial activities of the day, when extended mining revealed much about the earth's strata. It was at this period, the end of the eighteenth century, that James Hutton, the Scottish geologist, did so much to foster the growing interest in the science, while, in 1815, William Smith published the first geological map of England.

The new popular interest in nature and the wilder countryside meant not only a zeal for geology but also a renewed passion for botany. Many people began making their own collections of natural objects, and, as the seaside became increasingly popular at this time, these collections were often of shells—as Mr Knightley shows to the fragile Mr Woodhouse in Jane Austen's *Emma*, where

> *drawers of medals, cameos, corals, shells, and every other family collection within his cabinets had been prepared for his old friend.*

Most significant, however, was the way in which geology and other scientific movements of the age began, like Romanticism itself, to question the very fabric upon which society was built. As A. E. E. McKenzie explains in Volume 1 of his work *The Major Achievements of Science*:

> *There were repeated controversies between geologists and the upholders of the literal truth of Genesis, in which the whole future of Christianity was held by the latter to be at stake. The geologists eventually emerged victorious; the observation of nature triumphed over the revelation of scripture. It was established that the earth had not been created about 5,000 years ago, but that it had been in existence for millions of*

years; that Noah's flood was merely an episode in a series of great local inundations. . . . The widespread interest in the controversies was shown by the large sale of books on geology in the first half of the nineteenth century, and the result was a growth of scepticism in religion.

At the same time as such disputes were raging, came the first suggestion of theories of evolution. The poet Goethe, whose interest in nature led him to a detailed study of plants, drew a diagram showing how, in his opinion, plants had evolved; and Erasmus Darwin (grandfather of the Charles who was to create such a stir with his *On the Origin of Species by means of Natural Selection* in 1859) published in 1794–6 a work entitled *Zoonomia*, which suggested that life had evolved from a single source. These suggestions were of course anathema to those who believed in the Biblical version of creation, but they tie in with the idea so cherished by the Romantic poets of a unifying force binding all nature. Temporarily, at least, science and art seemed to go hand in hand.

✳   ✳   ✳

A much more obvious reflection of the Romantic mood in literature can be found in music of the period. As in the literary field, it was a time for breaking away from established custom and tradition, and for experimenting with new ideas. The chance to indulge in such musical innovation was severely restricted before this period by the reliance of musicians on patrons who commissioned works of a particular type for set occasions; but from the time of Beethoven (1770–1827), composers experimented widely, reflecting the Romantic desire for intellectual freedom.

Beethoven himself straddled the Classical and Romantic worlds, using the established form of sonata and symphony, but stretching the set framework to new limits. Even more significantly for the Romantic movement, he was an ardent republican, and many of his works reflect the struggle for freedom—particularly his only opera, *Fidelio*, which celebrates the fight of love and justice against tyranny.

The worship of the isolated Romantic hero in literature also found its reflection in music, in the delight of the growing middle-class public in exceptional virtuoso performers. The brilliant violinist Paganini, for example, who toured Europe in the early years of the nineteenth century, had such exceptional mastery of his instrument that he was said to be in league with the devil—to the delight of the crowds who flocked to see him. The pianist and composer Liszt was also fêted for his brilliant performance of works which were too difficult for others to master.

The Romantic delight in the individual expressed itself in a totally different form in the taste for intimate, personal songs. Both Schubert (1797–1828) and Schumann (1810–56) are most noted for their lyrical pieces, for their setting of contemporary poems to music in which piano and voice are subtly blended.

In complete contrast, this was also the era of the growing orchestra, when composers wishing to achieve new shades of feeling, or to express stronger emotions through music, wished to call on the resources of an orchestra containing more, and more accomplished, musicians. A highly imaginative work such as the *Symphonie Fantastique* by Berlioz (1803–69), for example, demands remarkable effects from the orchestra. This work is also, incidentally, typical of the new Romantic movement in music in that it tells a complete story, reflected at every stage by the music—a technique used more and more widely by composers at this period.

Music was being made to operate increasingly like a poem or a painting—to depict a scene from nature, to capture a mood, or to reflect an emotion. As the poet used words to express his own personal feelings which he hoped to share with his readers through the medium of imagination, so in exactly the same way the composer attempted to communicate his feelings. And as the aims of poets and composers grew closer, so it was no accident that musicians drew inspiration more and more frequently from Romantic writers. For example, Goethe's poems were frequently set to music by Schubert, while Liszt based his 'Faust' Symphony on Goethe's drama. Shakespeare, much admired by the Romantics, was also a recurrent source of inspiration, as in Mendelssohn's incidental music to *A Midsummer Night's Dream*, or Berlioz's *Béatrice et Bénédict*; while Liszt, following a taste for medieval poetry, wrote a 'Dante' Symphony.

More and more, as composers catered for the tastes of their middle-class audiences and not merely the whims of patrons, music reflected the popular tastes of the day—for the grotesque; for the revolutionary; and, very often, for the folk element, that *'language of men'* sought after in the literary field by poets such as Wordsworth. Schubert's songs reflect an awareness of folk tunes, and the opera *Der Freischütz* by Carl Maria von Weber (1784–1826) has a distinct folk element in its songs and dances. The 'natural'

rhythms of man as well as a love of natural beauty feature strongly in the music of the Romantic era.

*   *   *

But it is in the field of painting that the Romantic movement as seen in literature is most fully reflected. Both in Britain and on the continent came a desire for a more personal view of art, one which would express subjective truth with a new freshness.

In France, one of the earliest movements in this direction came from a painter who is at first sight Classical rather than Romantic—Louis David (1748–1825). But David's neo-classicism is in fact part of the revolutionary reaction against the extravagant corruption of the French *ancien régime*, and in its rejection of established values, and his search for a new, purer society, his work is in the full tide of Romanticism. The Napoleonic court deliberately echoed the days of ancient Rome in its choice of titles such as 'Consul', and then 'Emperor'; and David's paintings reflect the hope that France will see a return to honour and glory on the severe Roman model.

A picture such as his *Oath of the Horatii* (see Fig. 7) celebrates an event in Roman history where honour and love of the State are put before personal consideration. The picture is stark, simple, almost geometrical, allowing us to concentrate on the pure unselfishness of the heroes. A similar motive inspired his *Oath at the Tennis Court*, where modern republican sentiment is expressed in similarly uncluttered lines, suggesting single-minded dedication. And the painting *Death of Marat* is again stark, unelaborated, allowing us to concentrate on the cold fact of death, while the body of Marat lies like an ancient marble, cold and motionless.

But if Louis David represents the negative side of Romanticism —reaction against an established mode of society—he also represents one of its most forceful positive elements: worship of that isolated, exceptional man, the Romantic hero. In David's case, it was a particular man, Napoleon, whom he saw as rising above the common level and leading the masses to a new glory. In his painting of *Napoleon Crossing the Alps* we see the Emperor pointing onward and upward, symbolically mounting to greater heights: his cloak swirls forward, also pointing the way, and his horse rears up, eager to be on. It is not a portrait, but a vision—a vision of the Romantic superman.

However, Napoleon also represented for David the spirit of liberty from oppression which, at one time, he seemed to symbolize for all Europe. And this was a theme dear to the heart of all Romantic painters. Most notable perhaps, were the paintings of Delacroix (1798–1863) whose work *Liberty Leading the People* (see Fig. 8), depicting the overthrow of the Bourbon monarchy restored after the fall of Napoleon, suggests the continued fight of the French masses against tyranny. He also evoked the struggle of the Greeks against Turkish oppression in such paintings as *The Massacre at Chios* and *Greece Expiring on the Ruins of Missolonghi*. In Spain, Francesco Goya (1746–1828), who had spent his early years as a court painter, later depicted the horror and brutality of the French invasion of Spain in the early nineteenth century. Romantic artists, like Romantic writers, were fully conscious of the political struggles of their day.

In apparent contrast to this involvement with immediate events, another basic element of the Romantic movement, and one which we examined in detail in Chapter 7, was the interest in all things medieval, and in 'Gothic horror'. As the artists of the day reacted against the ordered rationality of eighteenth-century society, so their pictures reflected the growing interest in the strange, the exotic and the mysterious. Pictures of ruined abbeys, Gothic gateways and moonlit woods abound. The picture of *Crowland Abbey* by John Sell Cotman (1782–1842) is typical, with a silhouetted ruin looming up against dark, brooding clouds. J. M. W. Turner, the English artist who became most famous for his effects of light and colour, spent many of his earlier years examining the architectural delights of ruined abbeys such as Tintern (which also inspired the poet Wordsworth). His interest in the Gothic tracery can be clearly seen in pictures such as *Salisbury Cathedral: view from the Cloister*. Abroad, a similar delight in the melancholy, brooding aspects of Gothic can be found in the pictures of Caspar David Friedrich (1774–1840) where in such works as *Mountain Landscape with Rainbow* or *Man and Woman Gazing at the Moon* an intense light is used to throw into deeper contrast the gloomy rocks and trees which evoke an air of brooding mystery.

The interest in medievalism in literature meant a passionate delight in the works of Shakespeare, Milton and Dante and this too is reflected in paintings of the period. Dante's *The Divine Comedy* was fully illustrated by William Blake (1757–1827) and John Martin (1789–1854) produced illustrations for Milton's *Paradise Lost*. George Romney (1734–1802), John Runciman (1774–68), and Henry Fuseli (1741–1825) all illustrated Shakespearian plays, while at the same time fusing interest in his work with other aspects of Romanticism. Runciman's *King Lear in the Storm*, for example, is used as an opportunity to depict a raging sea, illustrating the interest at this period in the 'sublime' forces of nature, terrifying and amazing man; while Fuseli's *Lady Macbeth grasping the daggers* (see Fig. 19) is a deliberate choice of a horrifying subject, in keeping with the taste for the 'horror' novels of Mrs Radcliffe and Matthew Lewis. (The interest in Shakespeare as a representative of 'medieval' life, far removed from the squalid, colourless materialism of the early nineteenth century, was to continue as an inspiration for the next generation of British artists, the Pre-Raphaelites, as we shall see in the next chapter.)

The fact that 'scenes' from Shakespeare were, in reality, highly personal visions based loosely on the dramatic text, brings us to the point at which Romantic painting is most closely allied to literature. For the Romantic artist, the objective vision was of secondary importance; this is not to say that he was not a keen observer of the world around him, but his observations were distilled through his imagination, and he presented the world with a reality more intense than external fact could provide. Just as Keats felt that *'the imagination may be compared to Adam's dream—he awoke and found it truth'*; or as Shelley felt that the poet presented eternal truth, and was the ultimate lawgiver; so the Romantic painters produced works which faithfully reflected, not what they saw, but what they felt about what they saw.

The most extreme example is probably William Blake. Just as, in his poetry, he created his own mythological world, so in his pictures we see creatures of exaggerated power and intensity, often almost sculptural in the carved grandeur of their limbs or the stylized flow of their drapery. Figures such as *Nebuchadnezzar* or *Newton* (Figs 14 and 15) are not meant to be an attempt to capture 'real' personalities; nor is the 'scenery' meant to be convincingly true-to-life in *Dante and Virgil Approaching the Angel Who Guards the Entrance of Purgatory* (see Fig. 26), where the dark cloud hiding an intense radiance is symbolic. Blake is depicting an idea, not attempting to endue his pictures with photographic accuracy.

Samuel Palmer (1805–81) was much influenced by Blake, and his work conveys the same Romantic assertion that the artist's imagination is the only source of truth. His 'landscapes' conjure up not scenes, but atmospheres. The foliage is often larger than life, the moon has an intensity beyond the ordinary, and figures seem to fuse with the background to suggest a pattern of harmony. Like Blake, he seems to create a unified reality out of unreal exaggeration, and this is also true of the artist John Martin whose 'landscapes' are 'real' only through the dramatic intensity of their imagination.

This belief in the importance of the personal vision, however, did not always mean an imaginary reality. Sometimes it meant directing attention to certain aspects of external reality—selecting and refining objective truth, instead of depicting subjective perception only. Thomas Girtin (1773–1802) in his *The White House, Chelsea*, chooses to use the element of surprise in the startling reflection of the house to suggest the effect of light on water, creating a reality more intense than the eye would normally perceive. John Sell Cotman, whose *Crowland Abbey* we have already mentioned, in that picture paints a real place but infuses it with a particular atmosphere. In *Greta Bridge*, his technique is strict selectivity: he seems to choose only such features of the landscape as will form a rhythmic pattern. The rocks in the foreground carry the eye systematically through an irregular checkerboard of dark and light to the geometrically smooth arch and pointed parapet of the bridge in the distance, while the squareness of the house and the contrasting roundness of the trees carry the eye beyond and to each side. Nothing is superfluous detail: the solitary animal and herdsman serve to bring the eye back from the bridge to a triangle of lighter water—and hence to the rocks, and the foreground, to begin a new exploration of the pattern (Fig. 28).

28. *Greta Bridge* by J. S. Cotman. Cotman's paintings are notable for the way in which he imposes his own carefully selective vision on natural scenes. (British Museum, London)

But the genius of this type of personal vision, attempting to portray the kind of reality which only the artist is privileged to see, must be Joseph Mallord William Turner (1775–1851). It is the kind of genius which reminds us powerfully of the poetry of Shelley —often we perceive what he means with our senses, or at least with a part of our minds which is far removed from reason and logic. We could not paraphrase much of Shelley, any more than we could point to photographic reality in a Turner picture such as *Rain, Steam and Speed*, or *San Giorgio from the Dogana, Venice* (see Fig. 25). But we feel we know the kind of experience each is communicating.

If Turner's swirling, cloudy lights remind us of Shelley, his use of colour must evoke the poems of Keats. Just as Keats was fascinated by Italy for years before the final wretched months when he actually saw it, so Turner painted supposedly Italian scenes before visiting the country. But when he *did* visit it, he was fascinated, and the effect of glowing colour pulsating through brilliant light is seen clearly in his paintings of Italian landscapes. It is light and colour such as, perhaps, never existed, even in Italy, but it offers us the *effect* of Italy on Turner, just as Keats' poems can summon up for us the glowing colour and light of, say, Lamia's *'purple-linèd palace of sweet sin'*.

Another important influence which Keats and Turner share— and share with many Romantic poets and painters—is the sea. Turner shows it to us in all moods, smooth and glassy, wild and turbulent, blue and translucent, fiery and frothy. It is, perhaps, not surprising that the sea should so fascinate the Romantics; nothing could be a more powerful symbol of change, upheaval, inconstancy, sublimity—everything, in fact, which contrasted with the static, controlled landscape-garden atmosphere of the eighteenth century.

And yet not all artists of this period were fascinated by the stormy and the wild elements of landscape. One of the most famous of Romantic painters is the landscape artist, John Constable (1776– 1837). Constable painted the sea, as in *Weymouth Bay* or *The Sea near Brighton*. But what we instinctively think of when we recall his work are pictures of inland scenery, where, if there is water, it is the placid pool in front of *Dedham Mill*, or the gentle stream around *The Hay Wain*. And yet Constable's work is by no means static; the sense of movement is not Turner's swirling drama of the waves, but it is the equally compelling effect of the clouds, often scudding across hugely expansive skies and carrying the eye away with a sense of speed and urgency across the canvas.

29. *Hampstead Heath with a Rainbow* by John Constable. Constable creates a sense of dramatic spaciousness and movement in depicting the heath near where Keats once lived. (Tate Gallery, London)

Constable was one of several artists who raised landscape painting to a new height. Too often, landscape had meant a filling-in of background to a portrait or a stylized group of figures. But for Constable it was the most important aspect of art. Like Wordsworth, he drew from nature in its apparently simple aspects, and elevated the kind of scene one can still glimpse in most areas of England into a celebration of rural, anti-materialistic beauty. He saw poetry in simple, natural objects, as Wordsworth saw it in *'rustic life'* and *'the real language of men'*.

In this, Constable was not alone. Artists such as John Crome (1768–1821) in his *The Poringland Oak* could take a tree by a pool and, in depicting its convolutions in contrast to the stillness of the water and the smoothness of the bathers' bodies, suggest the power and endurance of nature (Fig. 30).

Even for painters such as Crome and Constable, however, the aspect of personal vision is important. Crome's tree dominates the scene because of the way he has chosen to place it, rearing up as a central, vertical line in contrast to the slightly undulating horizontals of the edges of the pool and the distant slopes. Constable's *Malvern Hall* seems swept to an immense distance by the darker, dominating trees, the broad expanse of sky, and by the upside-down reflection and repetition of the scene in the foreground lake. And in his *Hampstead Heath with a Rainbow*, Constable creates from the simple scene a sense of enormous space by his use of lines, first cutting the picture diagonally in the darker foreground, and then again horizontally in the lighter centre, above which clouds sweep across and the rainbow arches down, so every line compels our eye to centre on the starkly geometrical sails of the windmill (Fig. 29).

It is obviously true for every generation of artists and writers that what they depict is a personal vision. It was not a unique approach of the Romantic era. But, for the Romantics, it was an

30. *The Poringland Oak* by J. Crome. John Crome's painting exhibits both the interest at the time in a realistic study of nature, and a highly personal vision. Objective and subjective truth go hand in hand. (Tate Gallery, London)

approach which reached a new importance. Now, the individual imagination was not merely one element in creation—it was the most important element, transforming a scene glimpsed for a moment into a vision of everlasting truth, and a passing flash of light into infinite reality. As, for Keats, the spell of the Grecian urn was its ability to capture evanescent loveliness for eternity, so, for the Romantic painter, his canvas was the means by which he could catch for all time a momentary, visionary glimpse of absolute truth and beauty.

12

Later Writers and Painters

In their day, both Keats and Shelley were hounded by the critics—Keats for his poetry, Shelley for both his poetry and his extraordinary way of life. Today, both are accepted as great English poets and feature regularly on A-level examination syllabuses. Keats, who wanted to *'be among the English poets after my death'*, would presumably be pleased. Shelley, who always regarded himself as an inevitable outcast, would surely be incredulous.

And yet this fame and influence which escaped both poets during their brief lifetimes began to attach itself to their memories quite shortly after their deaths. Ironically, Keats and Shelley achieved some respectability at second hand through those two much-admired poets of the Victorian era, Robert Browning and Alfred Tennyson.

In 1826, the fourteen-year-old Browning requested his mother to buy him an edition of Shelley's poetry; not realizing quite what she was doing (for she was a devout Free Church woman) Mrs Browning complied. She also bought him the poems of Keats, and there is some evidence of Keats' influence on his poetry. But the influence of Shelley was immediate, startling and pervasive. Browning had been much affected by his mother's religious views; now he came face to face, intellectually speaking, with an avowed atheist and an acknowledged rebel. It was a stimulating and broadening experience. Later, he was to reject Shelley more and more, but, as William Irvine points out in *The Book, the Ring and the Poet*, Browning's early poems 'Pauline' and 'Paracelsus' owe much to Shelley's influence, and 'Pauline' in particular reflects quite closely 'Alastor' and 'Epipsychidion'.

In 'Pauline' which is written as an apparently autobiographical exploration of the poet's mind, Browning describes his childhood, *'passed alone with wisest ancient books'*, when he imagines himself the hero of the myths he read. Then came a time when he *'lost myself'*, but found consolation in poetry, both in reading *'the works of mighty bards'* and in writing his own verse. So he came across the works of one *'who was as calm as beauty'*. In Shelley (though Shelley is not specifically named), Browning found *'a key to a new world'*. He was inspired to a vision of what life could be, and it seemed glorious:

> *I was vowed to liberty.*
> *Men were to be as gods, and earth to heaven.*
> *And I—ah! What a life was mine to be,*
> *My whole soul rose to meet it.*[1]

But then he realized that this wonderful dream of what the world might be *was* only a dream, and not one he could bring to reality.

At this point in the poem we can begin to realize that Shelley is exerting a strange kind of double influence on the poet. Browning is both recalling the effect of Shelley on him, and at the same time borrowing the format of Shelley's 'Alastor' in which to do it. From this moment on, 'Alastor' and 'Pauline' run almost parallel. While the poet in 'Alastor' seeks the maid, Browning seeks a motive, a purpose in life. As the poet is compelled to voyage to seek his love, Browning finds he cannot shut himself away from the world, but must fuse with it. In a passage which reminds us forcibly of both Keats' and Shelley's ability to feel themselves part of Nature, Browning describes his sense of unity with the universe:

> *I can live all the life of plants, and gaze*
> *Drowsily on the bees that flit and play,*
> *Or bare my breast for sunbeams which will kill,*
> *Or open in the night of sounds, to look*
> *For the dim stars; I can mount with the bird,*
> *Leaping airily his pyramids of leaves*
> *And twisted boughs of some tall mountain trees.*
> *Or rise cheerfully springing to the heavens—*
> *Or like a fish breathe in the morning air*
> *In the misty sun-warm water—or with flowers*
> *And trees can smile in light at the sinking sun.*[2]

The poet in 'Alastor', after crossing the sea, reaches a wood, where

> *a well*
> *Dark, gleaming, and of most translucent wave*
> *Images all the woven boughs above,*
> *And each depending leaf, and every speck*
> *Of azure sky darting between their chasms.*[3]

The poet in 'Pauline' takes her, in thought, into a wood, where there is:

> *a small pool whose waters lie asleep*
> *Amid the trailing boughs turned water plants*
> *And tall trees over-arch to keep us in,*
> *Breaking the sunbeams into emerald shafts.*[4]

At this point where the poet in 'Alastor' sinks down in death, Browning reaches a crisis point too:

> *O God! Where does this tend—these struggling aims!*
> *What would I have?*[5]

But Browning resolves his crisis in a way that reminds us irresistibly of Shelley's 'Epipsychidion'. As Emily in that poem is to be Shelley's *'veilèd maid'*, so Browning feels that he will achieve new purpose with Pauline. He plans an idyll with her. They will go to her homeland,

> *Where nature lies all wild amid her lakes*
> *And snow-swathed mountains*[6]

where they will sit and sing and read, until Browning feels his soul renewed. Then he will be able to *'see all clearer and love better'*, and he will be able to make the spiritual progression he despairs of at the moment.

'Pauline' ends with a final invocation to the *'Sun-treader'*, whose inspiration he still needs, for, like Shelley, he has impossible tasks to perform, *'as one going in the dark to fight a giant'*. But now he is *'free from doubt or touch of fear'*.

It is obvious that in theme and ideas, Browning drew heavily from Shelley, and used much Shelleyan vocabulary and imagery. A cave, for example, is a common image in Shelley, often used, like Plato's in *The Republic*, to suggest an unenlightened or gloomy mind. In 'Pauline', Browning not only specifically refers to

> *the unshaped images which lie*
> *Within my mind's cave*[7]

but he also relates a dream where he was

> *a fiend, in a darkness chained for ever*
> *Within some ocean-cave.*[8]

There are obvious parallels here with 'Alastor', but an even closer parallel may be found in the strange tale narrated by Laone in 'The Revolt of Islam'; she too is taken to an underwater cave, *'pierced with one round cleft through which the sunbeams fell'*. There are other notable echoes of Shelley; Pauline must:

> *veil without a fear*
>   *That form,*[9]

reminding us not only of the *'veilèd maid'* of 'Alastor' but of the 'veil' image which we meet so frequently in Shelley—in, for example, the *'veilèd Divinity'* of 'Epipsychidion' or the *'subtle veil'* woven by the Witch of Atlas. And serpents, which occur so frequently in Shelley's poetry, also feature in 'Pauline'.

As Browning matured, his interest in Shelley lessened; however, it can still be seen in the theme of the blending of love and knowledge in 'Paracelsus'—again, reminiscent of the idea of 'Alastor', but also surely echoing the lessons of Goethe's *Faust*—and in 'Strafford', where tyranny is discussed and freedom and friendship debated. But if 'Pauline' is the poem of Browning's most clearly influenced by Shelley, it is perhaps not surprising when we recall that Browning was only twenty when he wrote it, and just of the age to be attracted by a rebellious, brilliantly gifted and tragically dead young poet.

31. *Alfred Lord Tennyson* by S. Lawrence, *c.* 1840. Tennyson, like Wordsworth, began his poetic career as a Romantic visionary, and ended it as a highly respectable Poet Laureate. (National Portrait Gallery, London)

Tennyson, too, was inspired as a young man by Shelley the *'Sun-treader'*. The poem 'The Poet' must surely refer to Shelley, echoing as it does the favourite Shelleyan images of fire, thunder, lightning and mountains, and eulogizing Freedom. We are inevitably reminded, too, of Shelley's experiments and enthusiasms when we read in Tennyson's 'The Princess' of the entertainments laid out on Sir Walter Vivian's lawns:

> *and here were telescopes*
> *For azure views; and there a group of girls*
> *In circle waited, whom the electric shock*
> *Dislink'd with shrieks and laughter;*
> *. . . a fire-balloon*
> *Rose gem-like up before the dusky groves*
> *And dropt a fairy parachute and past:*
> *. . . so that sport*
> *Went hand in hand with Science.*[10]

But though there are Shelleyan flashes in Tennyson, it is to Keats that he owes the greater debt.

Obviously, they both have an interest in medievalism. Keats' delight in Chaucer and Shakespeare is shared by Tennyson, and Gothic settings such as Keats uses in 'Isabella' or 'The Eve of St Agnes' provide the background to such poems as Tennyson's 'The Princess'—and, of course, all his Arthurian cycle. A shared interest does not prove an influence, however; but we can see the effect of Keats on Tennyson in numerous verbal parallels, too close to be purely coincidental, indicating that the later poet had read the earlier one with much attention and enjoyment. In 'The Princess', for example, the description of the picnic in the abbey ruins owes something to 'The Eve of St Agnes'. Keats describes *'a casement high and triple-arch'd . . . all garlanded with carven imag'ries'*, under which Porphyro sets a feast in *'baskets bright of wreathed silver'*. Tennyson writes of the ruins *'High-arch'd and ivy claspt'*, in which *'a feast Shone silver set'*.

Again, in 'The Palace of Art', we read of cloisters *'branch'd like mighty woods'*, reminding us of 'Hyperion', with

> *mighty woods,*
> *Tall oaks, branch-charmed by the earnest stars;*[11]

or in 'Oenone' it is impossible to avoid linking

> *many an inland town and haven large*
> *Mast-throng'd beneath her shadowing citadel*[12]

with the description in 'Ode on a Grecian Urn' of:

> *little town by river or sea shore,*
> *Or mountain-built with peaceful citadel.*

But the most important link between Keats and Tennyson is surely the often repeated idea, so central to them both, that art cannot be separated from life. Keats is often misunderstood in this connection, and, because he praises the imagination above *'consecutive reasoning'*, is thought to be rejecting reality. This is far from the truth; as we have seen, Keats felt passionately that the poet should embrace all experience with *'gusto'*, and that only by being fully aware of pain as well as pleasure, grief as well as joy, could the poet achieve maturity.

The temptation to avoid half of reality, by shutting out unpleasantness, was certainly one which Keats faced. In 'Ode on Indolence', for example, he tries to shut out the haunting image of love, ambition and poetry. In 'Ode to a Nightingale', too, he is tempted to shut out misery by drink, or even by death, but this is a passing mood. At his best moments, he knows that he must grasp all sensations fully, and leave behind the delights of pure fancy to come to grips with *'the agonies, the strife of human hearts'*. He must *'welcome joy and welcome sorrow'*, loving both *'fair and foul'*. In 'Ode on Melancholy', he asserts that contraries combine to make the richness of full experience:

> *Ay, in the very temple of Delight*
> *Veil'd Melancholy has her sovran shrine,*
> *Though seen of none save him whose strenuous tongue*
> *Can burst Joy's grape against his palate fine;*
> *His soul shall taste the sadness of her might,*
> *And be among her cloudy trophies hung.*

This belief is central to much of Tennyson's poetry, particularly his earlier work. Over and over again he rejects the idea that the artist can be the dreamer, living away from reality in a shadow world. This is at the heart of 'The Lady of Shalott'. The lady lives life at second hand, gazing through a mirror at reflections of reality— *'shadows'*, as she herself calls them. She has become accustomed to this, believing a curse will come upon her if she looks full at life. When she eventually does, tempted by the reflection of Sir Lancelot, and the protection of a secondhand existence is taken away (the mirror cracks), she cannot bear to face truth all the time, and dies.

32. *The Lady of Shalott* by William Holman Hunt. Tennyson's story of 'The Lady of Shalott' provides the Pre-Raphaelite painter Holman Hunt with a medieval setting full of strange, exotic detail. (City Art Gallery, Manchester)

The same insistence on a grasp of reality is at the centre of 'The Palace of Art', where the poet describes how he

> *built my soul a lordly pleasure-house,*
> *Wherein at ease for aye to dwell,*
> *I said, 'O soul, make merry and carouse*
> *Dear soul, for all is well.'*[13]

The pleasure-house is beautiful, decked with all the delights that the artistic mind or hand can invent, and at first the poet rejoices in his solitude. But, eventually, isolation becomes stagnation. The poet's soul grows dull, while vaguely aware of the full life of which it should be a part. He feels dead, mouldering, as if in a tomb, from which he can hear, far off, *'the dully sound of human footsteps fall'*. At last, the poet's soul leaves the beautiful but isolated pleasure-house to return to reality, vowing only to return to *'the Palace of Art'*, when he has learnt more of life; and vowing that, if he does return, it will never again be in isolation, but *'with others'*.

This theme also captured Tennyson in works such as 'The Lotos-Eaters', where the stranded seamen, eating the lotos which brings forgetfulness, abandon all thought of home and family, and all thought too of hardship and responsibility; as they recline on land, they give up for ever all thought of the sea (almost always an image of the Sea of Life in Tennyson's work) and accept the shadow for the reality:

> *Surely, surely slumber is more sweet than toil, the shore*
> *Than labour in the deep mid-ocean, wind and waves and*
> *oar.*[14]

In the poem 'The Princess', too, which might at first seem an early plea for women's education in the best Mary Wollstone-craft tradition, Princess Ida is really seen to be at fault. For she shuts herself away from half of life. Rejecting one extreme—the total subservience of woman to man—she opts for the other extreme. All men are barred from her territory, and she rejects all idea of love. When she learns that life cannot be lived in isolation, the Prince pledges himself to work with her for the spiritual richness that comes from total experience. And as the Princess learns, so does the Prince. He, like the Lady of Shalott, has been subject to a family curse, unable to tell *'The shadow from the substance'*, so that sometimes he *'seem'd to move among a world of ghosts'*, and felt himself *'the shadow of a dream'*. But Ida's love kills his doubts; together they learn to face the realities of life.

Tennyson, feeling that Art must share, and show, the experience of life—even if the setting were medieval, to show a richer, purer existence—chose to be far more didactic (that is, obviously teaching a moral lesson) than Keats, whose approach was more subtle. And this Tennysonian morality, together with a delight in things medieval and a Keatsian joy in colour, combine to form the basic elements of the Pre-Raphaelite Brotherhood, an artistic movement of the mid-nineteenth century, which owes a great deal to Keats.

The Brotherhood began in 1848 as a group of artists who rejected the formal, and as they saw it, sterile classical tradition, and who aimed at bringing a new vividness and reality to their paintings. There were seven original members, most important of whom were Dante Gabriel Rossetti (1828–82), John Everett Millais (1829–96) and William Holman Hunt (1827–1910). Later, as their ideas gained ground, other artists who seemed to be in the same tradition were also labelled Pre-Raphaelite.

The Pre-Raphaelites felt strongly the link between painting and literature, and as they were also greatly interested in medievalism, which they saw as offering a vision of a better, nobler world than that in which they lived, they frequently turned to literature which was either really of a bygone age—for example Dante or Shakespeare —or more contemporary writers who depicted medieval scenes, such as Keats (occasionally Byron) and Tennyson. Holman Hunt, for example, illustrated Shakespeare's *Measure for Measure* and Tennyson's 'The Lady of Shalott', while Millais illustrated *The Tempest, Hamlet,* Tennyson's 'Mariana' (itself based on *Measure for Measure*) and *Two Gentlemen of Verona.* They delighted in taking a scene from plays or narrative poems and depicting it as if the characters had been caught with all action momentarily suspended—the effect that would be achieved nowadays by taking a still from a ciné film. Such a scene they would reproduce with fanatical attention to detail, showing every line of an intricate tapestry pattern, every fold of a dress, even every leaf of a plant.

Keats' poems had an obvious appeal to artists with such tastes, for a poem such as 'The Eve of St Agnes', for example, is not only medieval in setting but full of magnificent verbal detail which could easily be transferred to the medium of paint on canvas, and it is also narrative from which a quintessential moment may be plucked. William Holman Hunt, who was already an avid enthusiast of Keats before meeting the other young artists with whom he was to form the Brotherhood, completed an illustration to the poem in 1848, showing Madeline and Porphyro fleeing the castle. (The same poem was to be illustrated as a triptych eight years later by the artist Arthur Hughes.) Another Pre-Raphaelite, Millais, completed in 1849 the painting which illustrates Keats' poem 'Isabella'. The lines of the poem it refers to provide no detail:

> *They could not sit at meals but feel how well*
> *It soothed each to be the other by*[15]

—but the picture captures the *essence* of Keats. It is, however, rather the Keats of 'Eve of St Agnes' than of 'Isabella', with the symbolic feast, the aged nurse, the damask cloth, and the lady in the cool, chaste grey we associate with Madeline, while Lorenzo wears the flame-colour associated with Porphyro (see Fig. 2 in Chapter 1).

Keats' passion for bright colour was of especial interest to the Pre-Raphaelites, who rejected the classical tendency for one main area of light surrounded by more shadowy patches, and concentrated on a glowing effect achieved by painting on top of a thin film of white. The brilliant luminosity of some of their work can be seen in such paintings as Ford Madox Brown's *The Pretty Baa Lambs* (1852) or John Brett's *The Stonebreaker* (1858).

Like Keats and Tennyson, the Pre-Raphaelites, even at their most medieval, felt strongly the need for art to be related to life. Like Shelley, whom they also admired, they felt that they were prophets, putting forward an inspired vision. Unfortunately, it was often a vision heavy with the kind of obvious didactic morality which sometimes mars the best of Tennyson. Pointed symbolism pushes home the message, as in Hunt's *The Awakening Conscience*, or Rossetti's *Found*, where the calf, pinned under a net and being driven to slaughter, makes an over-obvious parallel with the country-girl turned prostitute.

33. *Chatterton* by H. Wallis. The death of Chatterton provided the Pre-Raphaelite artist, Wallis, with a subject at once dramatic, sentimental and connected with literature and medievalism. (Tate Gallery, London)

At their best, however, the Pre-Raphaelites achieved a superb blend between art and reality, depicting, as Hogarth had done in an earlier age and different style, the social problems of their day. *Work*, by Ford Madox Brown, shows the value of labour. Equally, his *The Last of England* shows at once the wretchedness of the emigrants, the despair in their eyes, and yet the hope indicated by their fervently clasped hands as they set off to seek a new life; while in *Take Your Son, Sir!* Brown depicts without sentimentality the consequences of immorality.

Later, towards the end of the century, the interest in medievalism, combined with an intensification of reaction against the down-to-earth commercialization of the material world, led to less emphasis on contemporary social problems and a revival of the desire for 'Gothic' harmony. William Morris, friend and associate of the Pre-Raphaelites Rossetti and Madox Brown, started a business in wallpapers and furnishings decorated with the Gothic shapes and glowing natural colours which remind us forcibly of the ideas of Keats.

*   *   *

The direct influence of Keats and Shelley may thus be traced in English literature and art throughout the nineteenth century. But, more importantly, perhaps, than as an influence on their immediate successors, we should see them as the central point of a line of Romantic thought stretching back to the medieval Renaissance with its upsurge of humanism, and forward to the present day, where many of the ideals of Romanticism still flourish.

In Shelley's works, for example, the central, dominant image is surely the Promethean rebel—fiery, courageous, resisting oppressive authority from a consciousness of higher ideals and fiercely proud of the resistance. It is, basically, the image of humanism—of man battling proudly against apparently impossible odds, struggling vainly with either supernatural or tyrannous powers yet remaining glorious—that we can trace back ultimately to Greek tragedy. At the time of the Reformation, Luther himself, with his stern *'I can do no other'*, shows the same spirit of resistance, while Shakespeare's great tragic heroes, Macbeth, Hamlet and Lear, are all seen in some measure to be struggling against cosmic forces: *'As flies to wanton boys are we to the gods; They kill us for their sport.'* Milton's Satan, creation of a poet who was a rebel against King and established Church, censorship and conventional views on marriage, is a seventeenth century Prometheus. His name, *'Lucifer'*, light-bearer, shows his affinity with the fire-bringer, and also indicates his glory and splendour; for it is an essential of the Romantic hero that he is not merely a rebel, but a sacrificer. If he had little to lose, his resistance would be in some ways easier and less affecting. Satan has everything—an eternity of heaven—to lose, and has paradoxically chosen the omnipotent as his opponent. Like Shelley's Prometheus, his opposition seems hopeless, but he attempts it nevertheless.

There is, however, an essential difference here. Shakespeare's tragic heroes are largely themselves to blame for their own situations, by foolish or sinful action, and Milton's Satan, in spite of Blake's remark that Milton was 'of the Devil's party without knowing it', is quite clearly depicted as mean-spirited and bitter. Shelley's Prometheus stands out as a true 'Romantic hero' in that his motives are pure and altruistic. In this sense, the Shelleyan Romantic hero occurs rarely in literature. There is a glimpse of him in the novels of the Brontës, where Emily's Heathcliff represents the healthy freedom of nature against the stifling, consumption-ridden convention of the Lintons, but there is a cruel, evil streak in Heathcliff. And Charlotte's Mr Rochester shows other glimpses in his rejection of established law and custom, and ultimate suffering and purgation through fire and love, which are seen as more worthy than the apparent self-sacrifice of the priestly St John Rivers. But Rochester is far from altruistic.

A convincing Romantic hero, however, obviously in the Shelleyan mould, emerged in 1916 with the publication of James Joyce's *A Portrait of the Artist as a Young Man*, based on his earlier work, whose title clearly indicates his position, *Stephen Hero*. Stephen's surname is Dedalus—the name of the mythical artist who made wings for himself and his son Icarus to escape from the clutches of the tyrant Minos. Icarus flew too high, too near the sun, and perished. Joyce draws from the myth the images of creative art, escape from authority, and possible catastrophe through desire for new freedoms. Like Prometheus, and even more like Shelley, Stephen rejects the custom which stifles art and truth:

> *I will not serve that in which I can no longer believe, whether it call itself my home, my fatherland, or my church: and I will try to express myself in some mode of life or art as freely as I can and as wholly as I can . . . Welcome, O life! I go to encounter for the millionth time the reality of experience and to forge in the smithy of my soul the uncreated conscience of my race.*

As we shall see later in this chapter, the Romantic hero in this mould is still very much a sought-after ideal today.

*   *   *

If Shelley's ideals still pervade our thought, so in a more widespread way do the ideas of Keats. As we have seen, the elements of medievalism, of joy in colour and the senses, of vivid imagery, of the life of imagination, influenced Victorian literature. But the qualities of Keats also pervade poets whom we may regard as having a strong influence on modern poetry—for example, Gerard Manley Hopkins, whose poems, though of the Victorian era, remained unpublished until 1918, and had a profound effect upon the post-war movement.

Hopkins, like Keats, was deeply influenced by medieval verse. In Hopkins' case this influence, combined with an appreciation for the sound and the texture of words, led to an interest in the kind of alliterative poetry we associate with such early works as *Pearl* and *Sir Gawain and the Green Knight*. Yet it is not merely medieval; it is also that passion for moulding and stretching language to individual purposes which led the Romantics to revolt against classical restraint, and to aim for the intonations of natural speech against set forms. All these elements combine in a poem such as 'Binsey Poplars':

> *My aspens dear, whose airy cages quelled,*
> *Quelled or quenched in leaves the leaping sun,*
> *All felled, felled, are all felled;*
> *Of a fresh and following folded rank*
> > *Not spared, not one*
> > *That dandled a sandalled*
> > *Shadow that swam or sank*
> *On meadow and river and wind-wandering weed-winding*
> > *bank.*

The uniqueness of this style reminds us that Hopkins followed Keats in insisting on the intensity and importance of his own personal vision. Like Keats, he had an acutely observant eye for landscape, and upon this detailed observation his mind impressed its own patterns—the *'inscape'*, which we may compare with Keats' *'truth of imagination'*. Hopkins' journal reveals the intense delight in natural objects which we instinctively associate with the Romantic poets:

> *We have had other such afternoons, one today—the sky a*
> *beautiful grained blue, silky lingering clouds in flat-bottomed*
> *loaves, others a little browner in ropes or in burly-shouldered*
> *ridges swanny and lustrous.*[16]

> *I was looking at the high waves ... They are rolled out by the*
> *shallowing shore just as a piece of putty between the palms*
> *whatever its shape runs into a long roll. The slant ruck or*
> *crease one sees in them shows the way of the wind.*[17]

> *The rock is limestone, smooth and pale white, not rough and*
> *gritty, and without moss, stained red where the water runs*
> *and smoothly and vertically hewed by the force of the brook*
> *into high-walled channels with deep pools.*[18]

Another poet at the beginning of the modern period who follows in the Romantic tradition is unquestionably W. B. Yeats, who not only investigates such Keatsian problems as the value of art versus nature and dreams versus reality, but also explores the Romantic interest in medieval verse, especially the ballad form, simple, 'real' language, and the belief in the supernatural or 'faery'. The early lyrical poem, 'The Lake Isle of Innisfree' contains several phrases suggestive of Keats: 'the bee-loud glade'; 'evening full of linnet's wings'; 'lake water lapping with low sounds by the shore'. Later works, like 'The Tower', reflect the struggle between the life of imagination and abstract thought:

> *Never had I more*
> *Excited, passionate, fantastical*
> *Imagination, nor an ear and eye*
> *That more expected the impossible.*[19]

In his use of ballad form and old Irish legend, Yeats reflected a Wordsworthian Romanticism too—and that element of Romantic art and music which, in the nineteenth century, found expression in nationalism; for Yeats is essentially a poet of Ireland.

The Irish writer James Joyce, already mentioned as furnishing a true Romantic hero, follows verbally in the Romantic tradition too in his intense interest in the life of the senses and the inventive richness of his language, consciously investigated in the mind of Stephen Dedalus:

> *Words. Was it their colours? He allowed them to glow and*
> *fade, time after time: sunrise gold, the russet and green of*
> *apple orchards, azure of waves, the grey-fringed fleece of*

clouds. No, it was not their colours: it was the poise and balance of the period itself. Did he then love the rhythmic rise and fall of words better than their associations of legend and colour? Or was it that, being as weak of sight as he was shy of mind, he drew less pleasure from the reflection of the glowing sensible world through the prism of a language many-coloured and richly storied than from the contemplation of an inner world of individual emotions mirrored perfectly in a lucid supple periodic prose?

In the nineteen-twenties and thirties, this kind of interest in what may be called subjective language and the life of imagination gave way to an increased insistence on the actuality of things—how they appeared objectively—and to a social conscience which was concerned, perhaps inevitably in view of events at the time, with broad political and social issues. But the writings of Dylan Thomas (1914–1953) revealed a new interest in subjective, individual life, in imagery, in words as holding an innate delight for the poet, and once again a Romantic or neo-romantic movement came into vogue. The poem 'October Comes', for instance, published in the mid-forties by Edmund Blunden, reveals strong echoes of Gerard Manley Hopkins, especially the human transience theme of 'Spring and Fall', but takes us back ultimately to Keats' 'Ode to Autumn' and the insistence on savouring the joy of the moment. Blunden's alliterative images of autumn remind us of *'mists and mellow fruitfulness'*, as his *'crowns of cloud and thrones of light'* recall *'barred clouds bloom the soft-dying day'*.

*   *   *

And this interest in Romanticism, especially the Romanticism of Keats and Shelley, still has its influences today. In many ways—as was indicated at the beginning of Chapter 11—our attitudes are still influenced by the attitude of the great era of the Romantics. Like Shelley, the younger generation over the last twenty years has drawn its heroes from rebels—not necessarily altruistic rebels, it is true, but the individual standing out against the establishment, whether in the field of entertainment or politics. The adulation of James Dean or Che Guevara, for example, stems from the desire to see the individual as more important than the society of which he forms a part. It is a viewpoint which has pervaded all aspects of western society from education to prison reform, and which is perhaps one of the strongest elements of a supposedly 'free' society.

The desire to 'do one's own thing'; the right to 'speak one's mind'; and the complete freedom of the media—these are all in complete opposition to totalitarianism in any shape or form, and are all attitudes dear to the mind of the nineteenth-century Romantics, especially Shelley. At the same time, we live in an age of great central control, where the State has much bureaucratic power and where even acts of alms-giving are no longer performed on a personal basis but run by organized teams, who use the media to rouse a mass social conscience. In this way, we are at the centre of two massively opposed forces—the demands of society and the needs of the individual. Strangely enough, this was exactly the situation in which the world—and Keats and Shelley—found itself at the turn of the nineteenth century.

The Romantic poets spent their lives trying, through their writings, to fuse and harmonize these two elements. Whether they succeeded or not, they still have much to say to us about the struggle; and to that extent, this is still the age of Keats and Shelley.

[1] Robert Browning 'Pauline' 425–428   [2] ibid. 716–26   [3] 'Alastor' 457–61   [4] as 1, 752–55   [5] ibid. 811–12   [6] ibid. 952–3   [7] ibid. 969–70   [8] ibid. 99–100   [9] ibid. 45–6   [10] Alfred, Lord Tennyson 'The Princess' 67–70; 74–6; 79–80   [11] 'Hyperion' Book I, 73–4   [12] Alfred, Lord Tennyson 'Oenone' 116–17   [13] Alfred, Lord Tennyson 'The Palace of Art' 1–4   [14] Alfred, Lord Tennyson 'Song of the Lotos-Eaters' VIII   [15] 'Isabella' I, 5–6   [16] Gerard Manley Hopkins (ed. by Humphrey House) The Journals and Papers of Gerard Manley Hopkins (O.U.P., 1959) p. 207   [17] ibid. p. 223   [18] ibid. p. 235   [19] W. B. Yeats 'The Tower' 4–7

Bibliography

This is not intended to be an exhaustive bibliography; a search of the shelves of any good library or bookshop will reveal numerous works of interest to the student of Keats and Shelley not mentioned in this short list. It is hoped, however, that this bibliography may be used as a starting-point for the reader who wishes to delve further into the background of the period, and who would like some indication of where to begin.

BIOGRAPHICAL AND AUTOBIOGRAPHICAL MATERIAL ON KEATS AND SHELLEY

Keats
BATE, W. J.   *John Keats* (O.U.P., 1963)
FAUSSET, H. I. (ed.)   *Letters of John Keats* (Nelson, 1938)
GITTINGS, R.   *John Keats: The Living Year* (Heinemann, 1954) and *John Keats* (Heinemann, 1968)

Shelley
BRAILSFORD, H. N.   *Shelley, Godwin and their Circle* (O.U.P., 1954)
CLARK, D. L. (ed)   *Shelley's Prose* (University of New Mexico Press, 1954)
GLOVER, A. S. B. (ed.)   *Shelley: Selected Poetry, Prose and Letters* (Nonesuch Press, 1951)
HOLMES, R.   *Shelley—The Pursuit* (Weidenfeld & Nicolson, 1974)
JOHNSON, R. B. (ed.)   *Letters of Shelley* (Bodley Head, 1929)
PEACOCK, T. L.   *Memoirs of Shelley* (Hart-Davis, 1970)
The Life of Percy Bysshe Shelley (2 vols.) (Dent, 1933)   This contains *The Life of Shelley* by T. J. Hogg, *Recollections of Shelley and Byron* by E. J. Trelawny and *Memoirs of Shelley* by T. L. Peacock

ORIGINAL BACKGROUND SOURCES: ESSAYS, LETTERS, POETRY AND NOVELS

Before the Seventeenth Century
AESCHYLUS (trans. by P. Vellacott)   *Prometheus and Other Plays* (Penguin, 1964)

BOCCACCIO, GIOVANNI (trans. by G. H. McWilliam)   *The Decameron* (Penguin, 1972)

DANTE ALIGHIERI (trans. by G. L. Bickersteth)   *The Divine Comedy* (Aberdeen University Press, 1955)

DANTE ALIGHIERI   *The Vita Nuova and Canzoniere of Dante Alighieri* (Dent, 1948)

PLATO (trans. by W. Hamilton)   *The Symposium* (Penguin, 1951)

PLUTARCH (trans. by I. Scott-Kilvert)   *The Rise and Fall of Athens* (Penguin, 1970)

Seventeenth to Mid-eighteenth Century
CHESTERFIELD, P. D. S.   *Letters of Lord Chesterfield to his Son and Others* (Dent, 1935)

GRAY, THOMAS   *Selected Letters of Thomas Gray* (O.U.P. 1951)

HENDERSON, P. (ed.)   *Shorter Novels of the Seventeenth Century* (Dent, 1967)

ROUSSEAU, JEAN JACQUES (ed. by F. Watkins)   *Political Writings* (Nelson, 1953)

ROUSSEAU, JEAN JACQUES (trans. by G. D. H. Cole)   *Social Contract and Discourses* (Dent, 1927)

Mid-eighteenth Century to Mid-nineteenth Century
BEWICK, THOMAS   *Memoir. Written by Himself* (Bodley Head, 1925)

BURKE, EDMUND   *On Taste; On the Sublime and Beautiful* (Collins, New York, 1937)

BURKE, EDMUND   *Speeches and Letters on American Affairs* (Dent, 1955)

BURKE, EDMUND (ed. by Conor Cruise O'Brien)   *Reflections on the Revolution in France* (Penguin, 1969)

CHATTERTON, T. (ed. by H. D. Roberts)   *Complete Poetical Works* (2 vols) (Routledge, 1906)

COBBETT, WILLIAM   *Rural Rides* (Penguin, 1967)

COLERIDGE, SAMUEL TAYLOR (ed. by Shawcross)   *Biographia Literaria* (2 vols) (O.U.P., 1939)

GODWIN, WILLIAM   *Political Justice* (Allen and Unwin, 1929)

GOETHE, JOHANN WOLFGANG (trans. by P. Wayne) *Faust Part One* (Penguin, 1961)

GOETHE, JOHANN WOLFGANG (trans. by W. Rose) *The Sorrows of Young Werther* (Scholartis Press, 1929)

HAYDON, BENJAMIN ROBERT *Autobiography and Journals* (Macdonald, 1950)

HAZLITT, WILLIAM *Table Talk* (Dent, 1936), *Lectures on the English Poets* and *The Spirit of the Age* (Dent, 1951)

JOHNSON, SAMUEL (ed. by E. L. McAdam and G. Milne) *Johnson's Dictionary: a Modern Selection* (Gollancz, 1963)

JOHNSON, SAMUEL (ed. by M. Wilson) *Prose and Poetry* (Hart-Davis, 1963)

MALTHUS, T. *Essay on the Principle of Population* (Macmillan, 1966)

OWEN, ROBERT *The Life of Robert Owen* (Charles Knight, 1971)

PAINE, THOMAS (ed. by Bonner) *Common Sense and the Crisis* (Watts and Co., 1949) and *The Rights of Man* (Watts and Co., 1949)

RADCLIFFE, ANNE (ed. by B. Dobrée) *Mysteries of Udolpho* (O.U.P., 1966)

SMITH, ADAM *The Wealth of Nations* (2 vols) (Dent, 1950)

SMITH, DAVID NICHOLL (ed.) *Oxford Book of Eighteenth Century Verse* (O.U.P., 1926)

SOUTHEY, R. (ed. by J. Simmons) *Letters from England* (The Cresset Press, 1951)

WAIN, J. (ed.) *Contemporary Reviews of Romantic Poetry* (Harrap, 1953)

WORDSWORTH, WILLIAM (ed. by P. Wayne) *Letters of Wordsworth* (O.U.P., 1954)

Three Gothic Novels (Penguin, 1968) Contains *Vathek* by W. T. Beckford, *The Castle of Otranto* by H. Walpole and *Frankenstein* by Mary Shelley

HISTORICAL BACKGROUND: MODERN WORKS

BRIGGS, A. *The Age of Improvement* (Longman, 1959)

COWIE, L. C. *Hanoverian England 1714–1837* (Bell and Sons Ltd, 1967)

DEANE, P. *The First Industrial Revolution* (Cambridge University Press, 1965)

HOBSBAWM, E. J.   *Industry and Empire: from 1750 to the Present Day* (Penguin, 1969)   (vol. 3 of Penguin Economic History of Britain)

HOBSBAWM, E. J.   *The Age of Revolution* (Weidenfeld and Nicholson, 1962)

NICHOLSON, H.   *The Age of Reason* (Panther, 1969)

PLUMB, J. H.   *England in the Eighteenth Century, 1714–1815* (Penguin, 1950)   (vol. 7 of Pelican History of England)

THOMPSON, E. P.   *The Making of the English Working Class* (Penguin, 1968)

TREVELYAN, G. M.   *Illustrated English Social History* (vols 3 and 4) (Penguin, 1960)

WATSON, S.   *The Reign of George III* (O.U.P., 1960)   (vol. 12 of the Oxford History of England)

WILLEY, B.   *Seventeenth Century Background* (Penguin, 1962) and *Eighteenth Century Background* (Penguin, 1962)

BACKGROUND TO ART, MUSIC, SCIENCE, ETC.

BERNAL, J. D.   *The Scientific and Industrial Revolutions* (vol. 2 of *Science in History*) (Penguin, 1969, also C. A. Watts and Co., 1965)

BRION, M.   *Art of the Romantic Era* (Thames and Hudson, 1966)

CLARK, K.   *Civilisation* (BBC Publications, 1969)

CLARK, K.   *The Gothic Revival* (John Murray, 1967)

HALL, A. F.   *The Scientific Revolution 1500–1800* (Longman, 1967)

HAUSER, A.   *Rococo, Classicism and Romanticism* (vol. 3 of *The Social History of Art*) (Routledge, 1962)

HILTON, T.   *The Pre-Raphaelites* (Thames and Hudson, 1970)

MACKENZIE, A. E. E.   *The Major Achievements of Science*, (vol. 1) (Cambridge University Press, 1960)

PEVSNER, N.   *An Outline of European Architecture* (Penguin, 1961)

RICH, A.   *Music, Mirror of the Arts* (Pitman, 1970)

ROBERTSON, A. and STEPHENS, D.   *Classical and Romantic* (vol. 3 of the Pelican History of Music) (Penguin, 1969)

POETICAL WORKS

BLAKE, WILLIAM   *Poems and Prophecies by William Blake* (Dent, 1939)

BROWNING, ROBERT   *The Poetical Works of Robert Browning* (O.U.P., 1957)

BYRON, GEORGE GORDON   *The Poems of Byron* (O.U.P., 1964)

KEATS, JOHN (ed. by J. M. Murray)   *The Poems and Verses of John Keats* (Eyre and Spottiswoode, 1949)

POPE, ALEXANDER (ed. by J. Butt)   *The Poems of Alexander Pope* (Methuen, 1963)

SHELLEY, PERCY BYSSHE (ed. by T. Hutchinson)   *The Poems of Shelley* (O.U.P., 1961)

TENNYSON, ALFRED (ed. by C. Ricks)   *The Poems of Tennyson* (Longman, 1969)

WORDSWORTH, WILLIAM   *The Poetical Works of Wordsworth* (O.U.P., 1956)

Index

Page numbers in italics refer to illustrations.